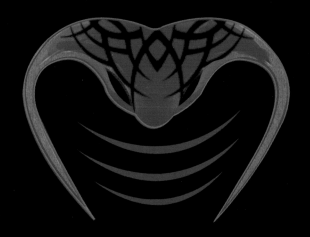

THE KAURAVA EMPIRE

EMPIRE

VOL. 1

ABHIMANYU AND THE CONQUEST OF THE CHAKRAVYUHA

CAMPFIRE®

KALYANI NAVYUG MEDIA PVT LTD

THE KAURAVA EMPIRE

VOL. 1

ABHIMANYU AND THE CONQUEST OF THE CHAKRAVYUHA

WRITTEN BY: JASON QUINN
ILLUSTRATED BY: SACHIN NAGAR
COLOURIST: SACHIN NAGAR
EDITORS: JASON QUINN, SOURAV DUTTA
DESIGN: ERA CHAWLA
LETTERING: BHAVNATH CHAUDHARY

www.campfire.co.in

Published by Kalyani Navyug Media Pvt Ltd
101 C, Shiv House, Hari Nagar Ashram,
New Delhi 110014, India

ISBN: 978-93-80741-89-5

Copyright © 2014 Kalyani Navyug Media Pvt Ltd

Printed in India

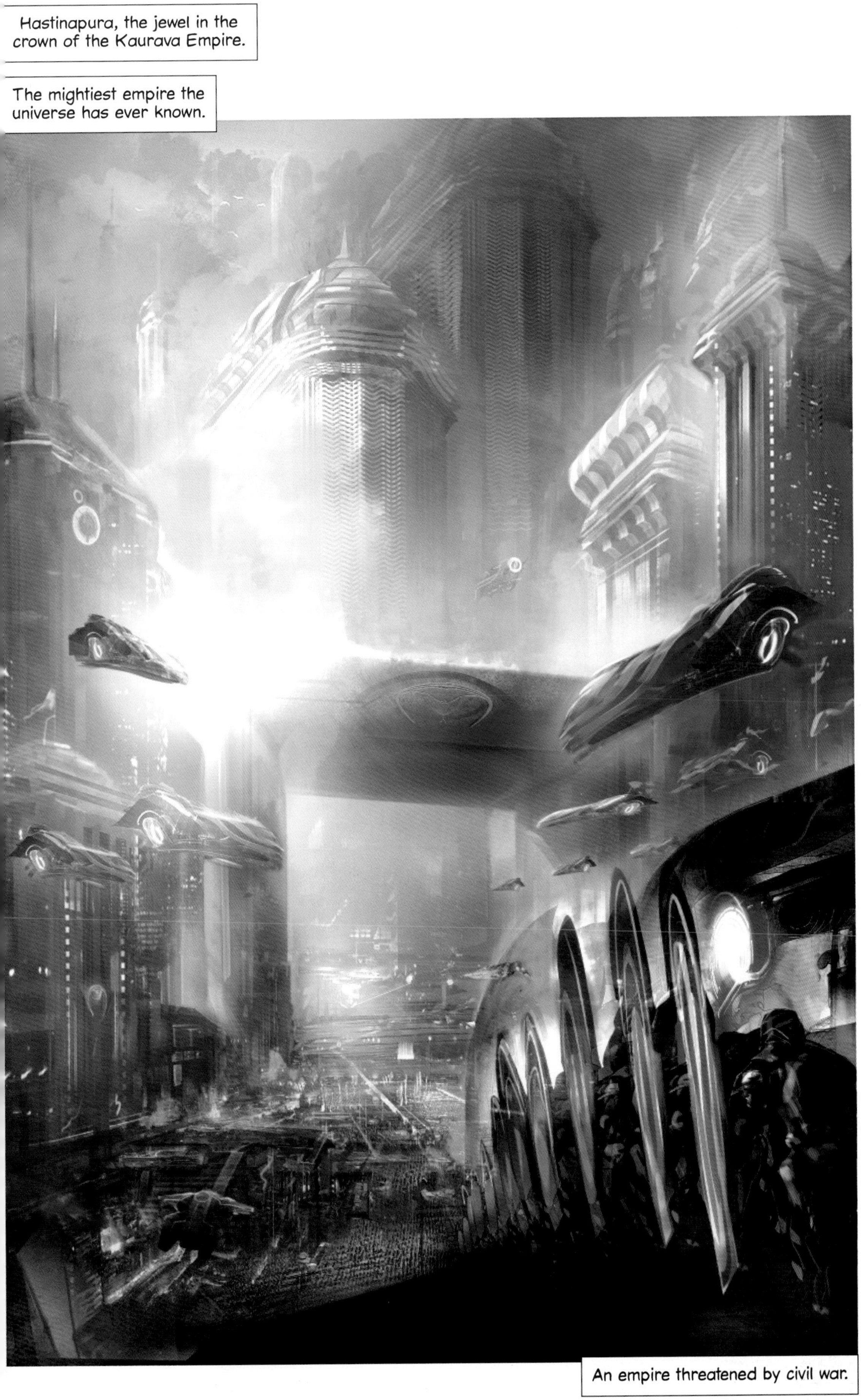
Hastinapura, the jewel in the crown of the Kaurava Empire.
The mightiest empire the universe has ever known.
An empire threatened by civil war.

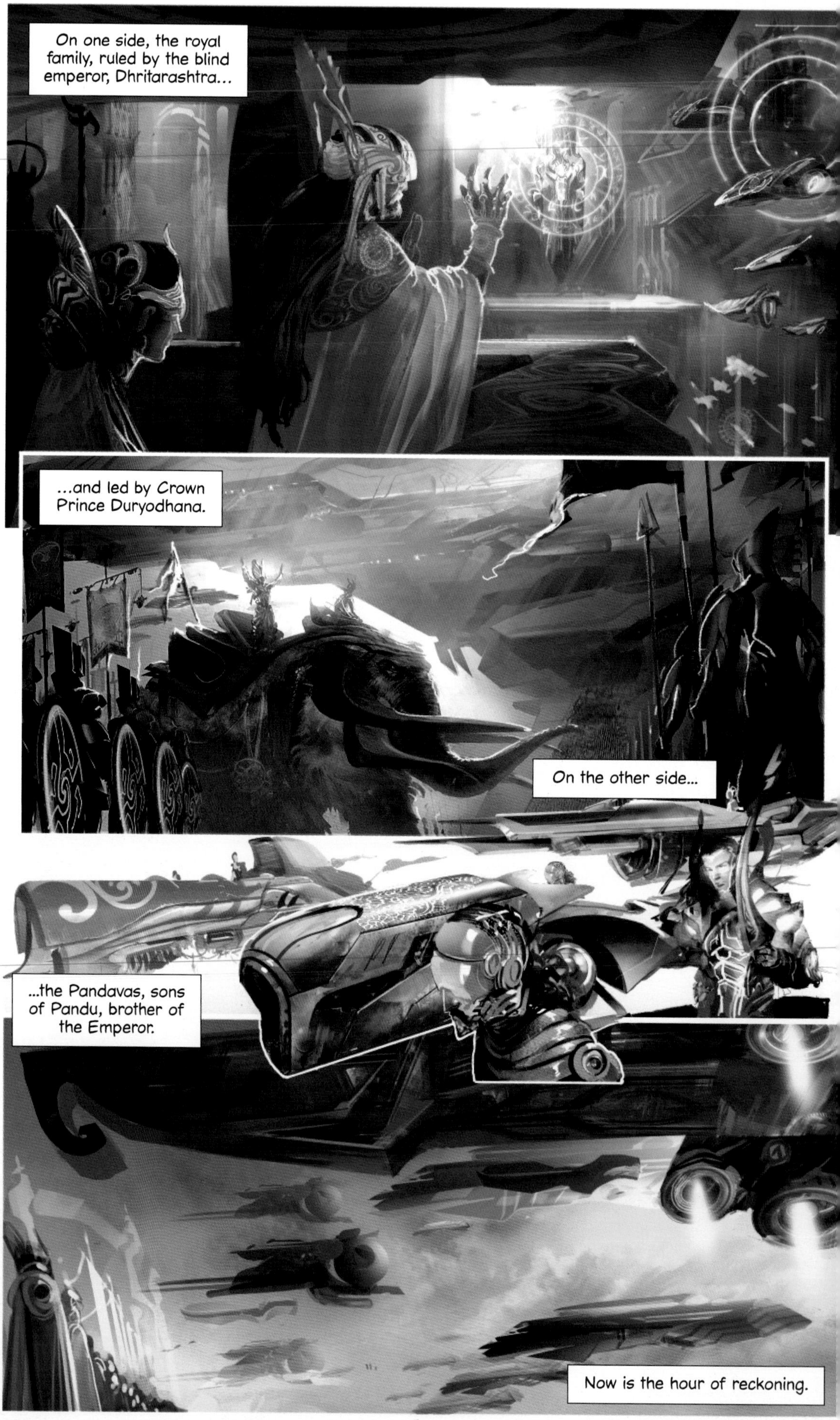
On one side, the royal family, ruled by the blind emperor, Dhritarashtra...
...and led by Crown Prince Duryodhana.
On the other side...
...the Pandavas, sons of Pandu, brother of the Emperor.
Now is the hour of reckoning.

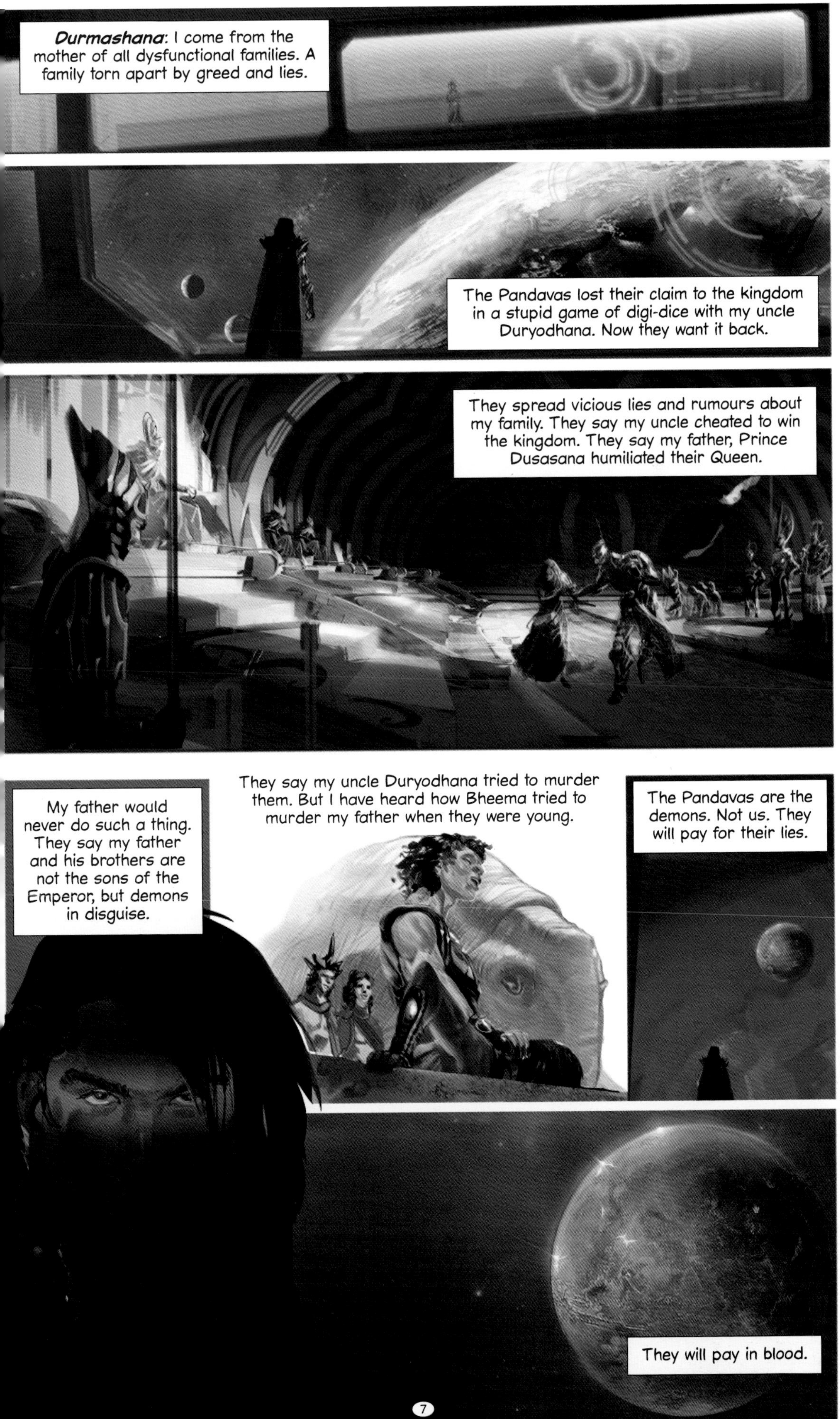
Durmashana: I come from the mother of all dysfunctional families. A family torn apart by greed and lies.
The Pandavas lost their claim to the kingdom in a stupid game of digi-dice with my uncle Duryodhana. Now they want it back.
They spread vicious lies and rumours about my family. They say my uncle cheated to win the kingdom. They say my father, Prince Dusasana humiliated their Queen.
My father would never do such a thing. They say my father and his brothers are not the sons of the Emperor, but demons in disguise.
They say my uncle Duryodhana tried to murder them. But I have heard how Bheema tried to murder my father when they were young.
The Pandavas are the demons. Not us. They will pay for their lies.
They will pay in blood.

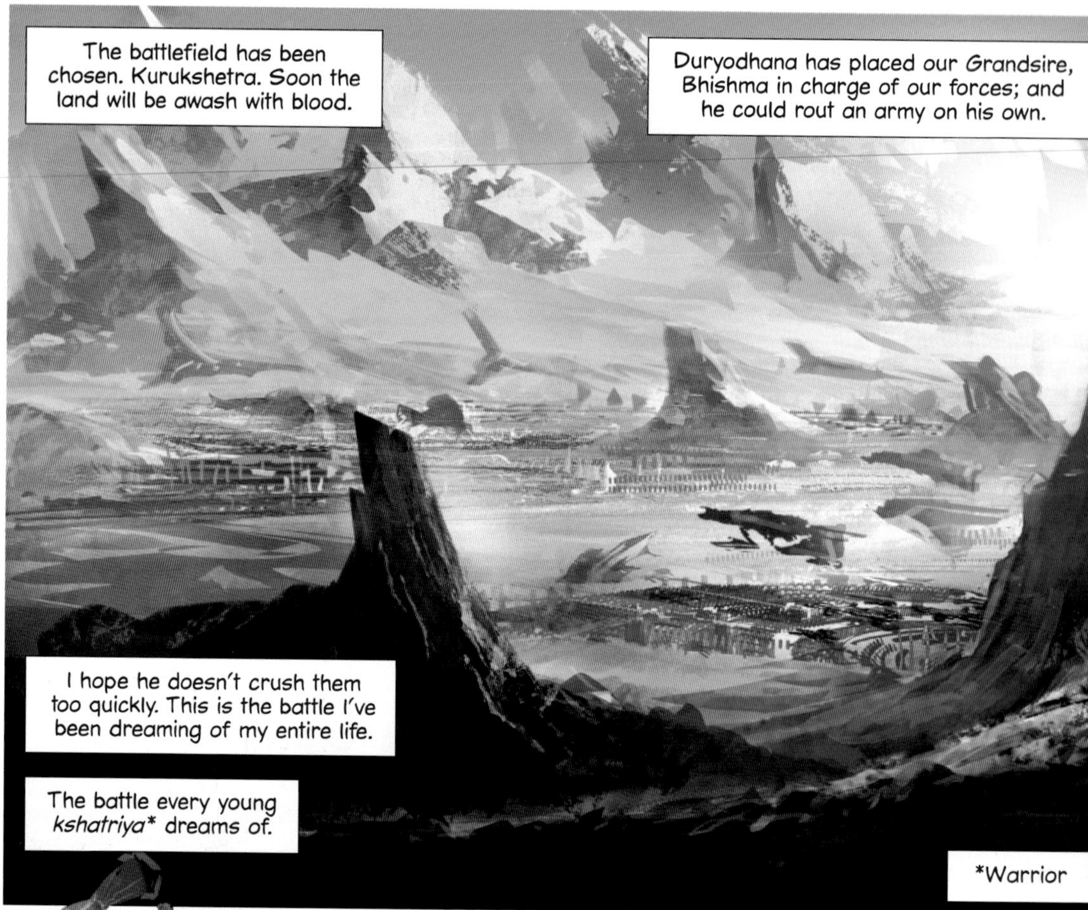
The battlefield has been chosen. Kurukshetra. Soon the land will be awash with blood.
Duryodhana has placed our Grandsire, Bhishma in charge of our forces; and he could rout an army on his own.
I hope he doesn't crush them too quickly. This is the battle I've been dreaming of my entire life.
The battle every young *kshatriya** dreams of.
*Warrior

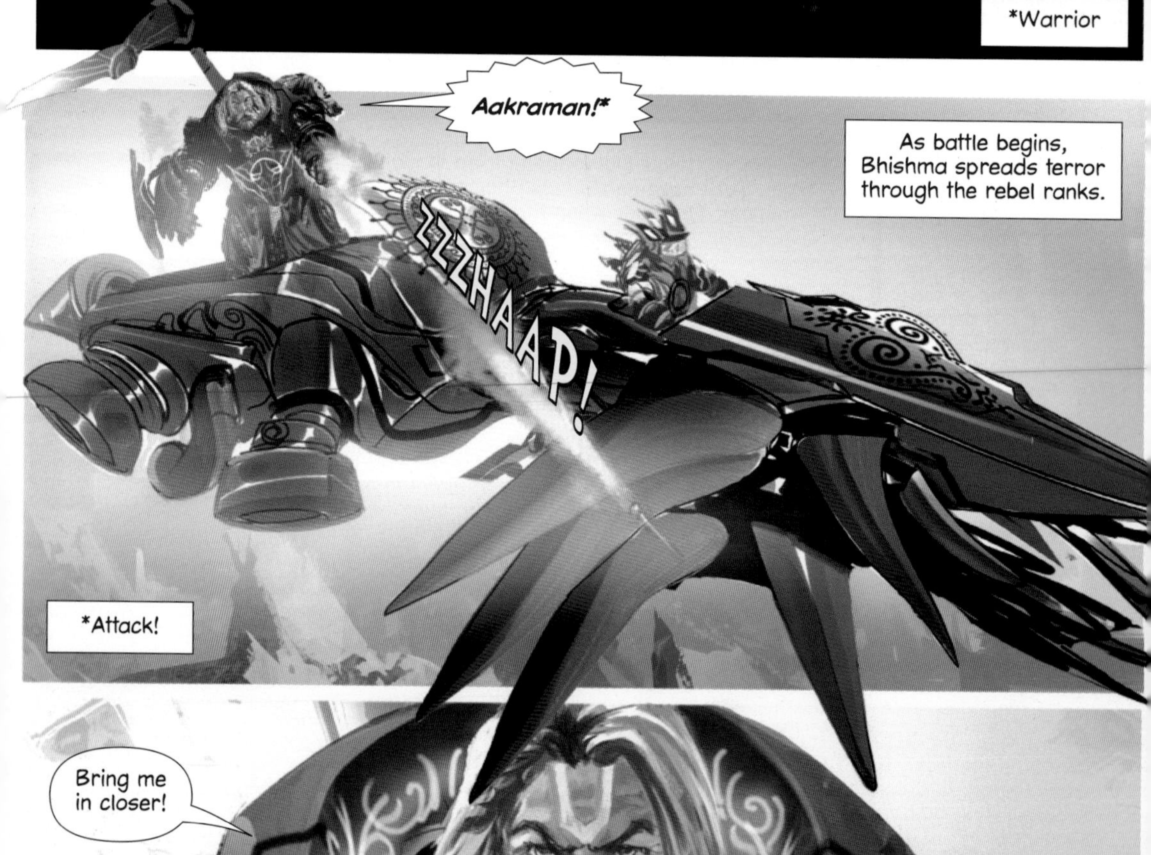
Aakraman!*
As battle begins, Bhishma spreads terror through the rebel ranks.
ZZZHAAAP!
*Attack!

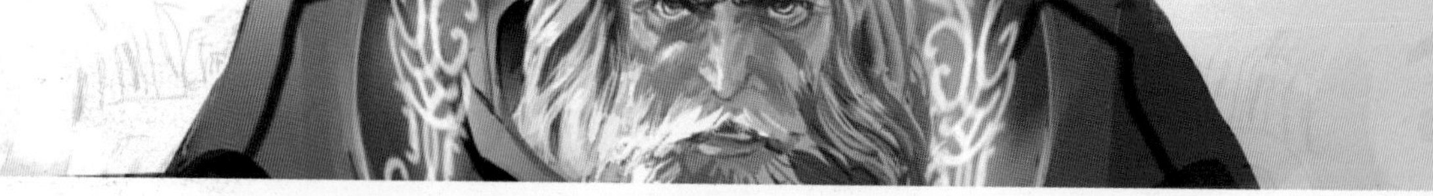
Bring me in closer!

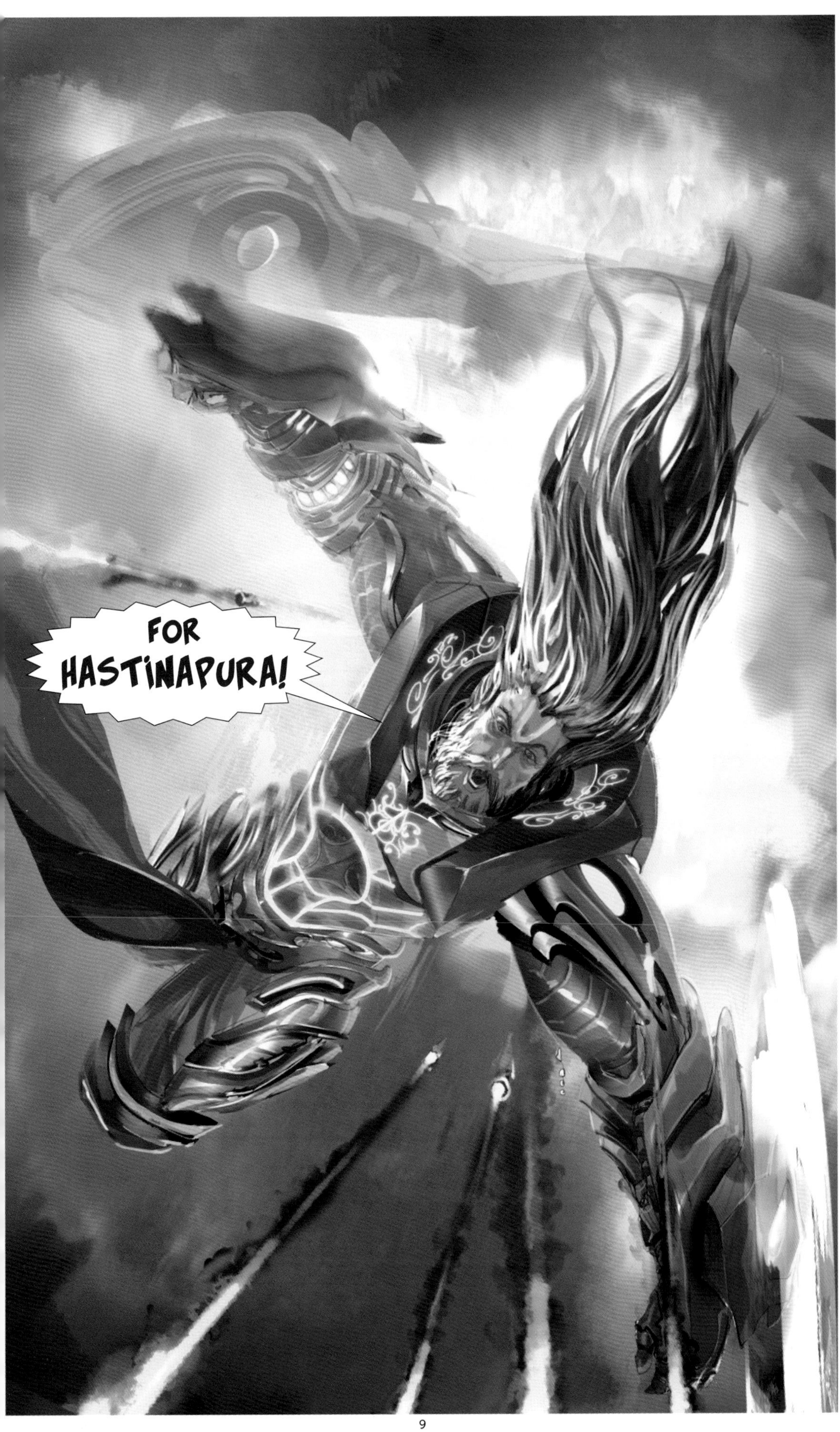
FOR HASTINAPURA!

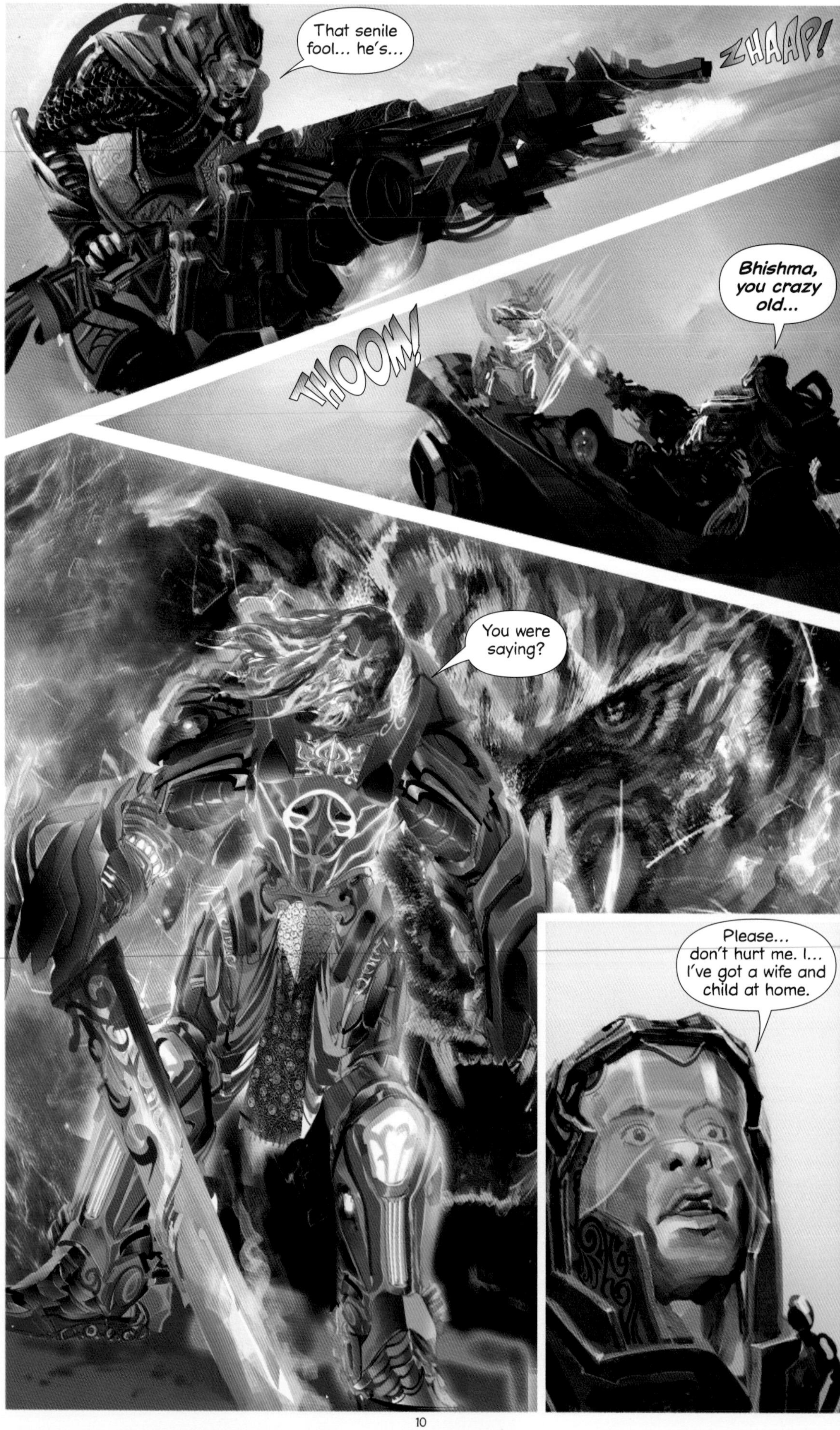
That senile fool... he's...
ZHAAP!
Bhishma, you crazy old...
THOOM!
You were saying?
Please... don't hurt me. I... I've got a wife and child at home.

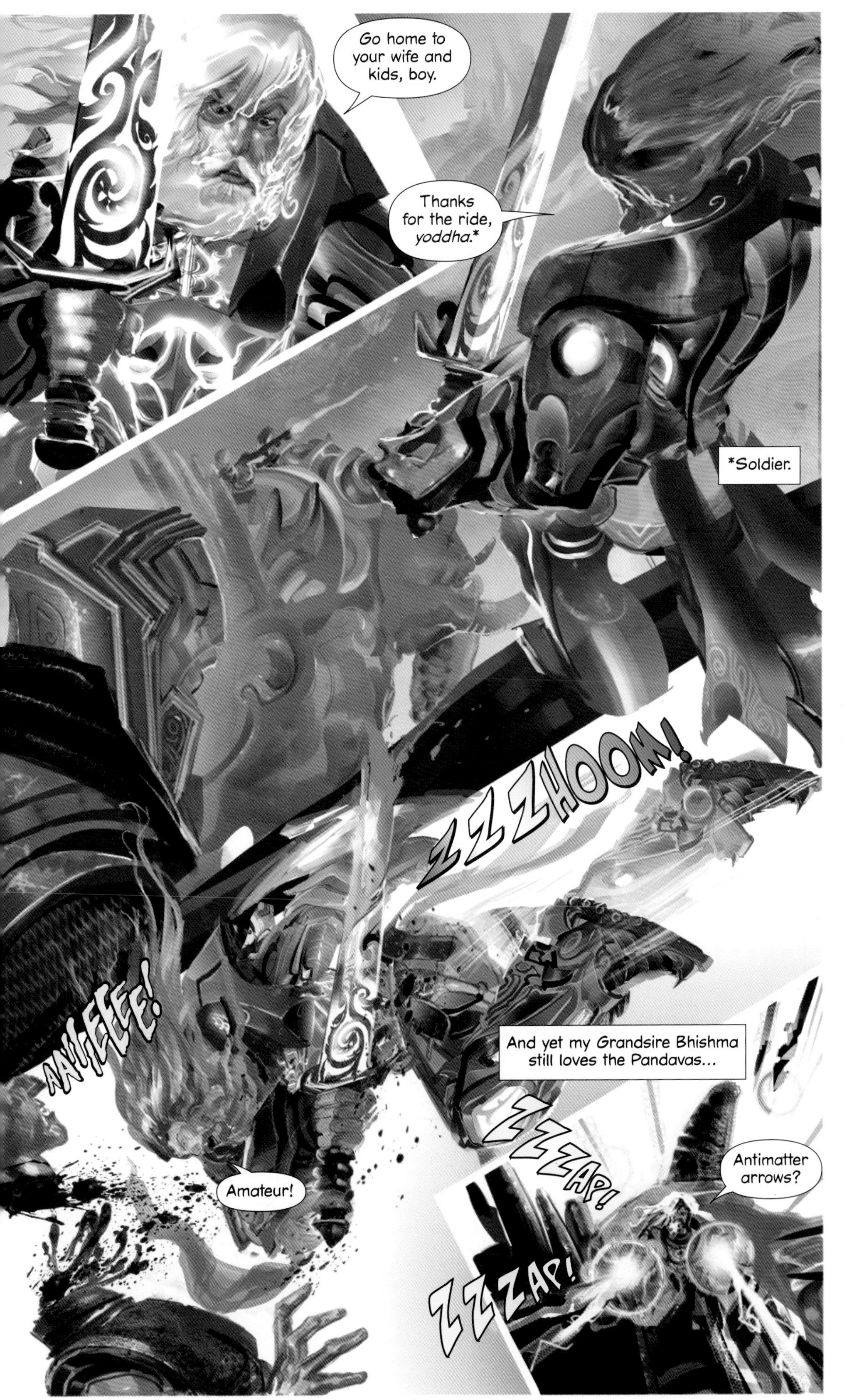
Go home to your wife and kids, boy.
Thanks for the ride, *yoddha.**
*Soldier.
ZZZHOOM!
AAIIEEEE!
And yet my Grandsire Bhishma still loves the Pandavas...
Amateur!
ZZZAP!
Antimatter arrows?
ZZZAP!

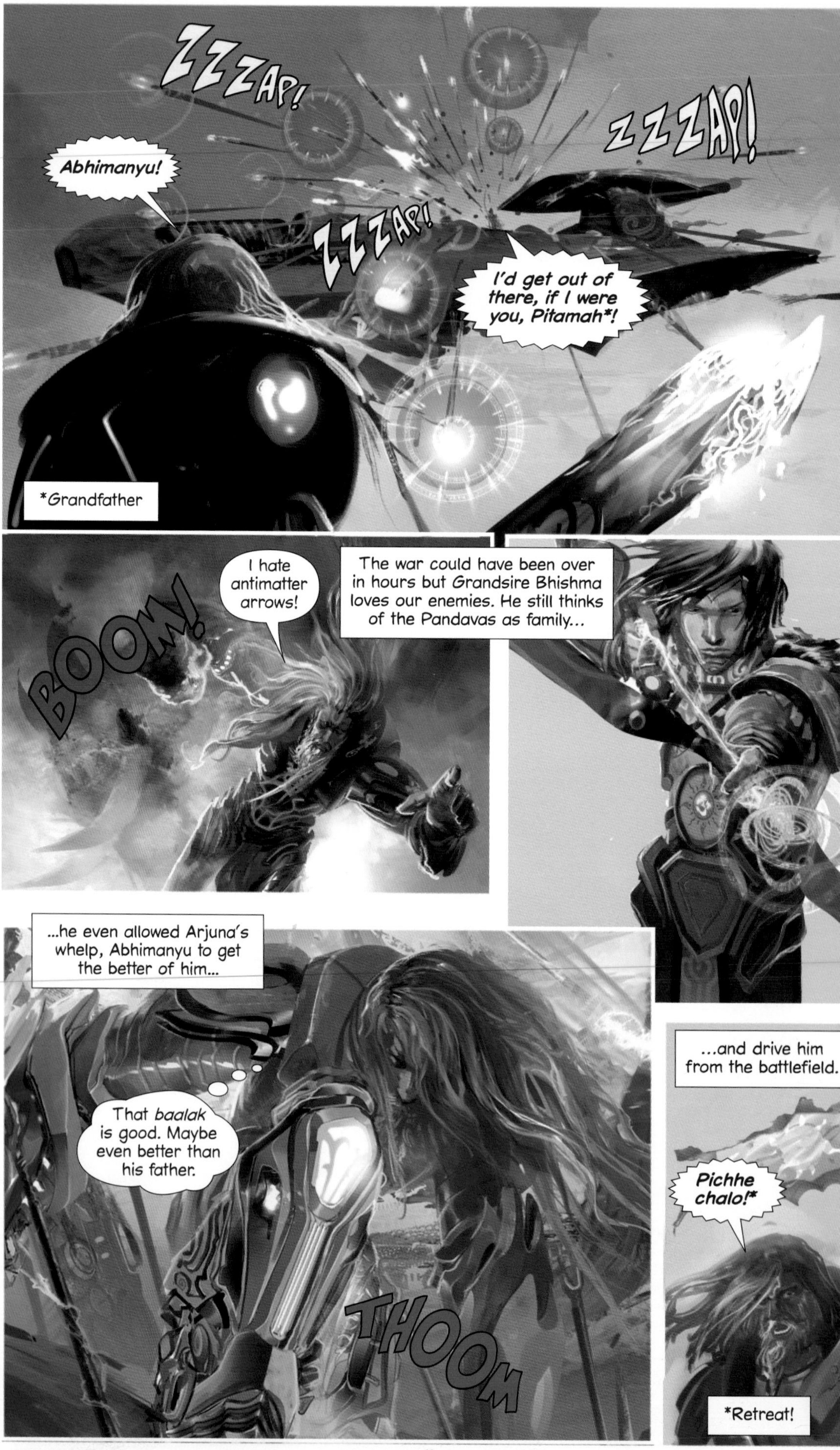
ZZZAP!
ZZZAP!
Abhimanyu!
ZZZAP!
I'd get out of there, if I were you, Pitamah*!
*Grandfather
BOOM!
I hate antimatter arrows!
The war could have been over in hours but Grandsire Bhishma loves our enemies. He still thinks of the Pandavas as family...
...he even allowed Arjuna's whelp, Abhimanyu to get the better of him...
That baalak is good. Maybe even better than his father.
THOOM
...and drive him from the battlefield.
Pichhe chalo!*
*Retreat!

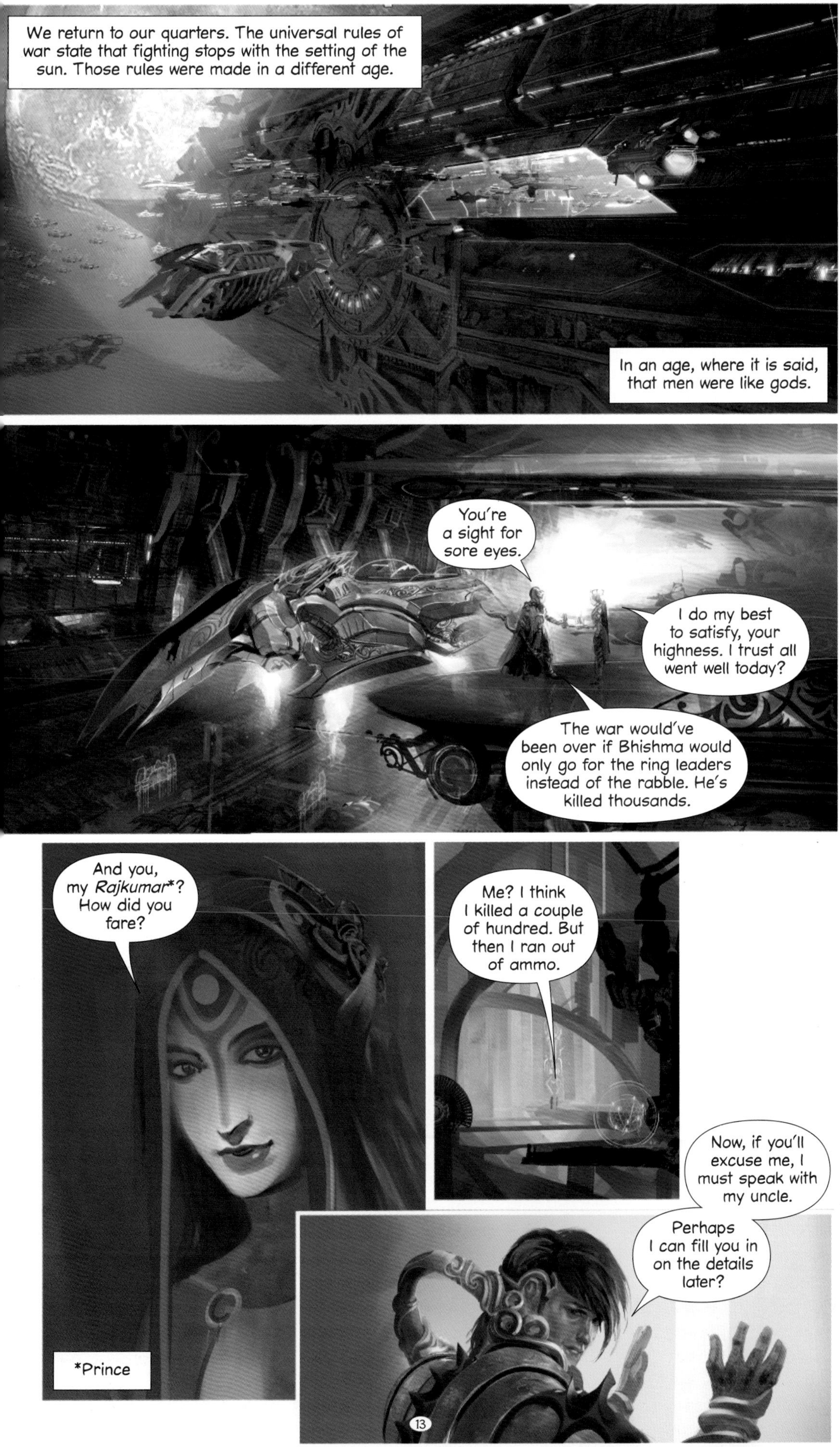
We return to our quarters. The universal rules of war state that fighting stops with the setting of the sun. Those rules were made in a different age.
In an age, where it is said, that men were like gods.
You're a sight for sore eyes.
I do my best to satisfy, your highness. I trust all went well today?
The war would've been over if Bhishma would only go for the ring leaders instead of the rabble. He's killed thousands.
And you, my *Rajkumar**? How did you fare?
*Prince
Me? I think I killed a couple of hundred. But then I ran out of ammo.
Now, if you'll excuse me, I must speak with my uncle.
Perhaps I can fill you in on the details later?

My uncle, Duryodhana is in high spirits, as are most of our forces.

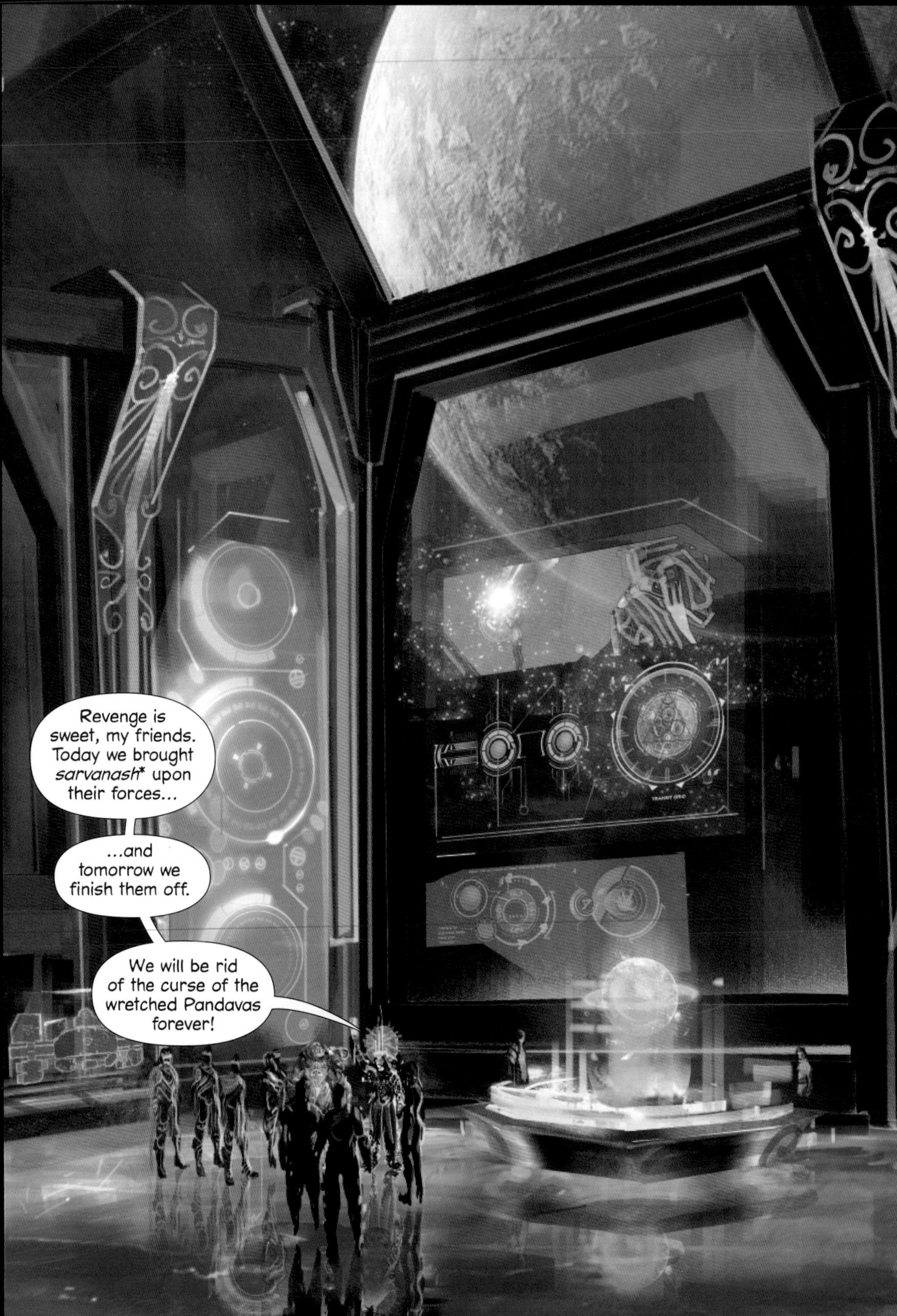
Revenge is sweet, my friends. Today we brought *sarvanash** upon their forces...
...and tomorrow we finish them off.
We will be rid of the curse of the wretched Pandavas forever!

*Destruction

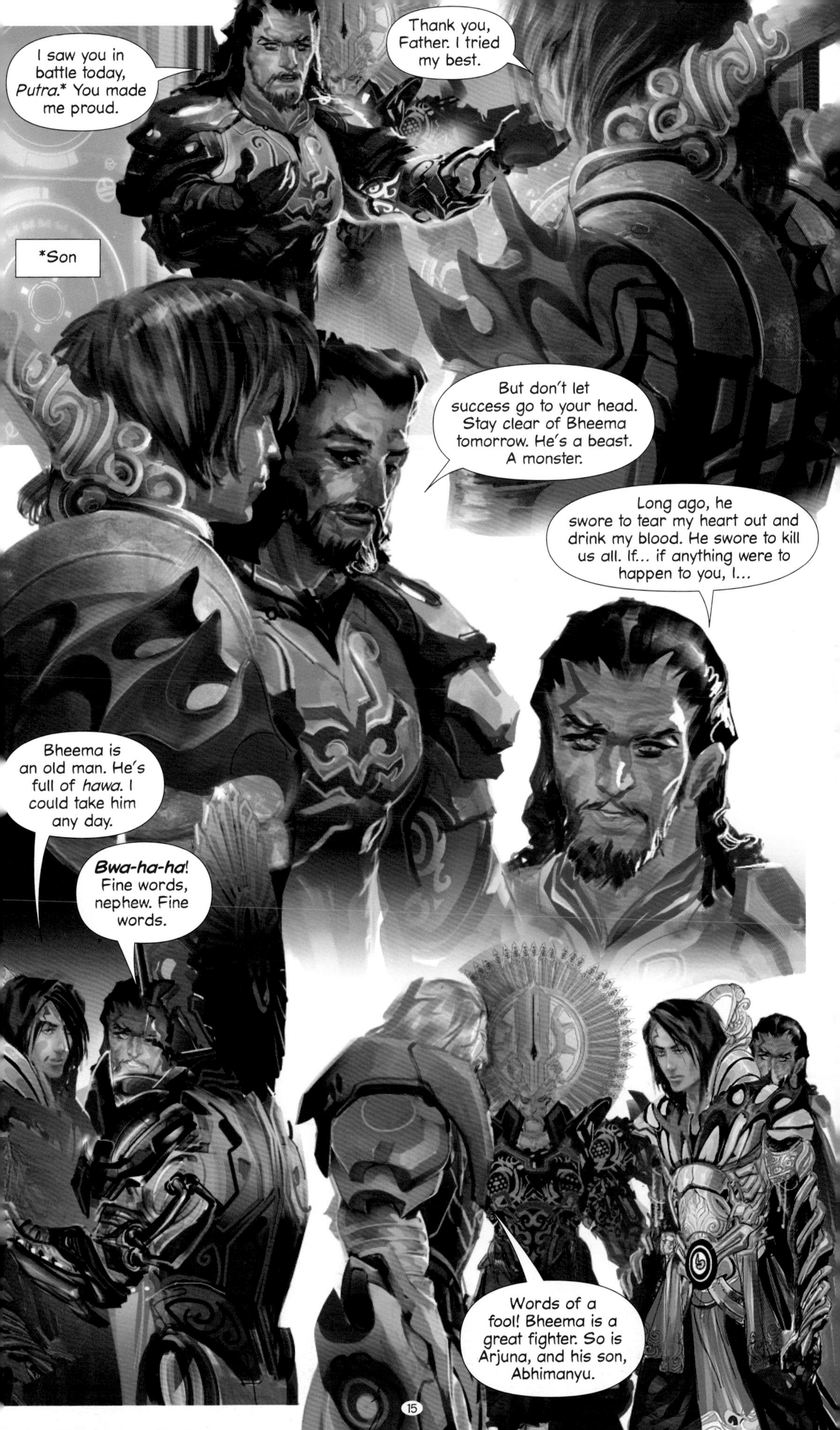
I saw you in battle today, *Putra.** You made me proud.
Thank you, Father. I tried my best.
*Son
But don't let success go to your head. Stay clear of Bheema tomorrow. He's a beast. A monster.
Long ago, he swore to tear my heart out and drink my blood. He swore to kill us all. If... if anything were to happen to you, I...
Bheema is an old man. He's full of *hawa*. I could take him any day.
Bwa-ha-ha! Fine words, nephew. Fine words.
Words of a fool! Bheema is a great fighter. So is Arjuna, and his son, Abhimanyu.

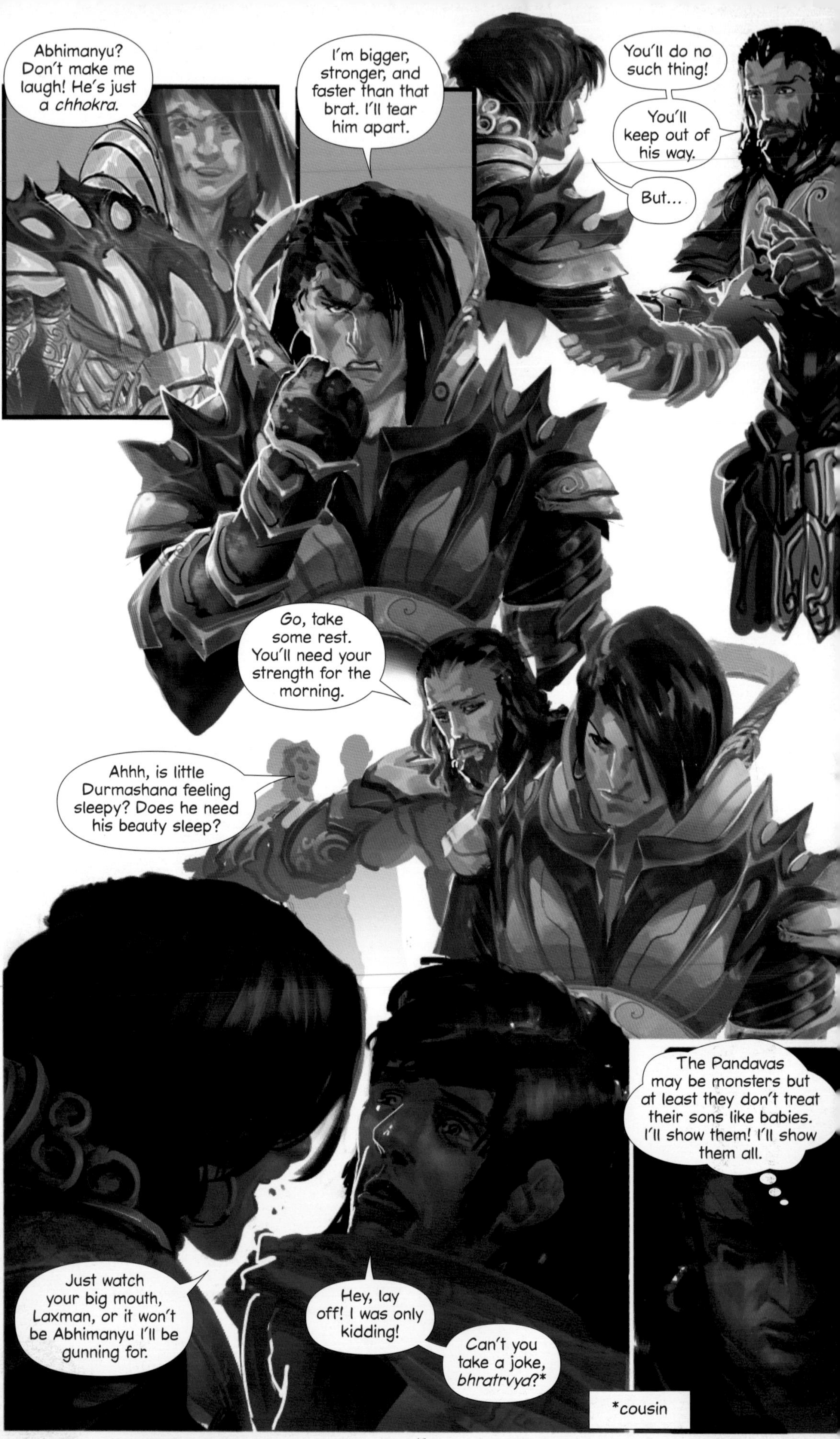

Abhimanyu? Don't make me laugh! He's just a *chhokra.*
I'm bigger, stronger, and faster than that brat. I'll tear him apart.
You'll do no such thing!
You'll keep out of his way.
But...
Go, take some rest. You'll need your strength for the morning.
Ahhh, is little Durmashana feeling sleepy? Does he need his beauty sleep?
Just watch your big mouth, Laxman, or it won't be Abhimanyu I'll be gunning for.
Hey, lay off! I was only kidding!
Can't you take a joke, *bhratrvya?**
The Pandavas may be monsters but at least they don't treat their sons like babies. I'll show them! I'll show them all.
*cousin

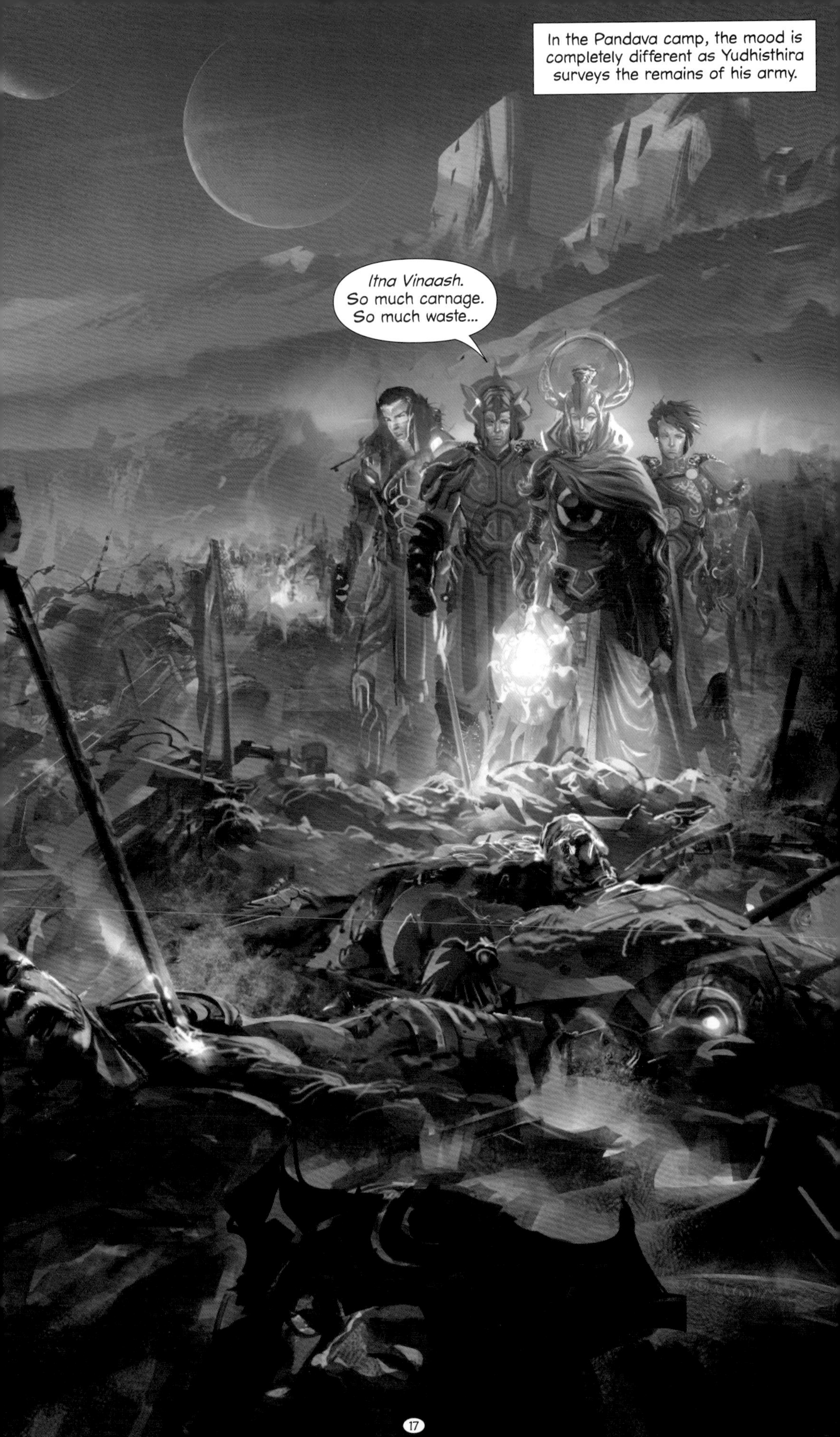
In the Pandava camp, the mood is completely different as Yudhisthira surveys the remains of his army.
Itna Vinaash. So much carnage. So much waste...

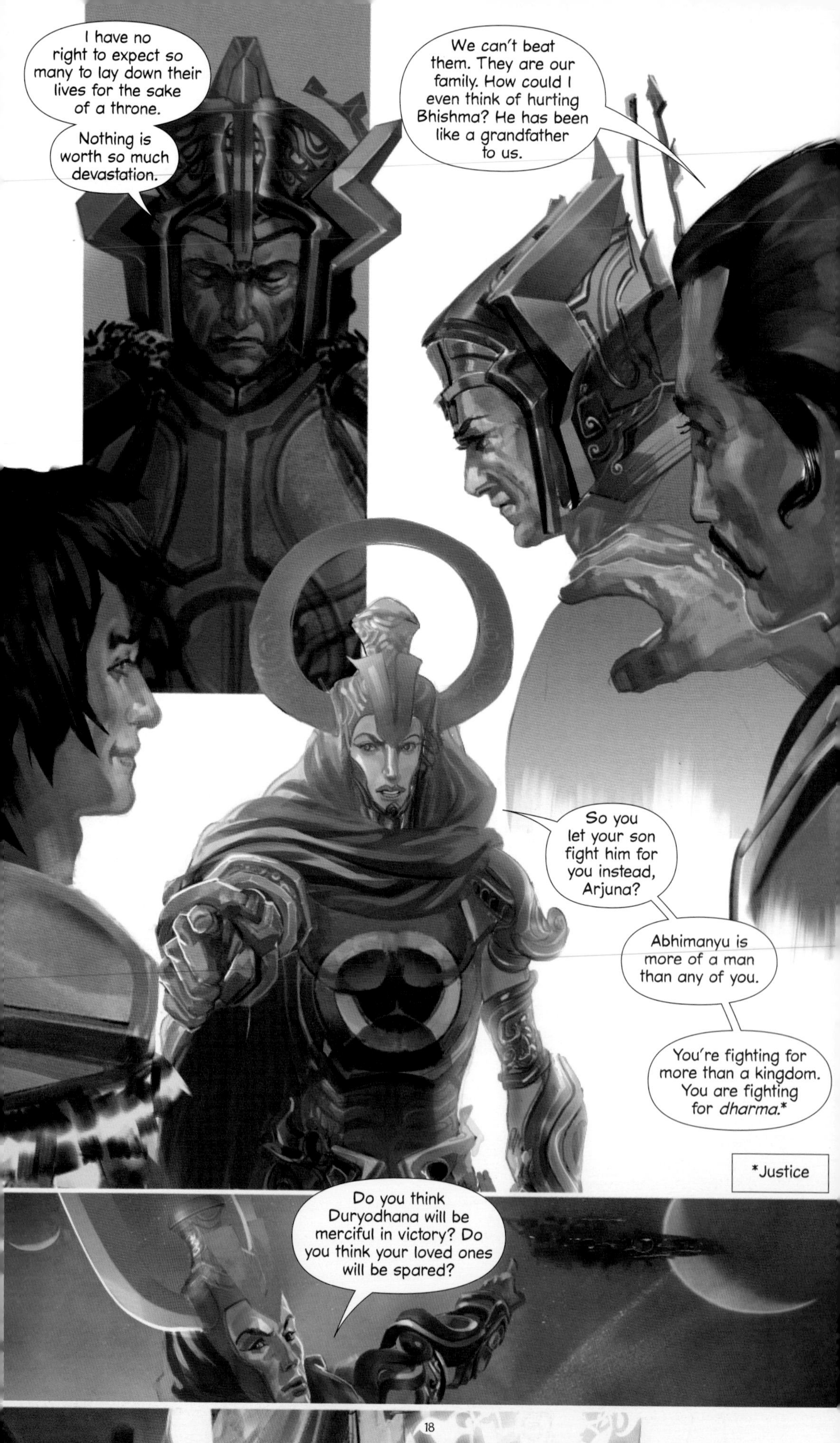
I have no right to expect so many to lay down their lives for the sake of a throne.
Nothing is worth so much devastation.
We can't beat them. They are our family. How could I even think of hurting Bhishma? He has been like a grandfather to us.
So you let your son fight him for you instead, Arjuna?
Abhimanyu is more of a man than any of you.
You're fighting for more than a kingdom. You are fighting for *dharma.**
*Justice
Do you think Duryodhana will be merciful in victory? Do you think your loved ones will be spared?

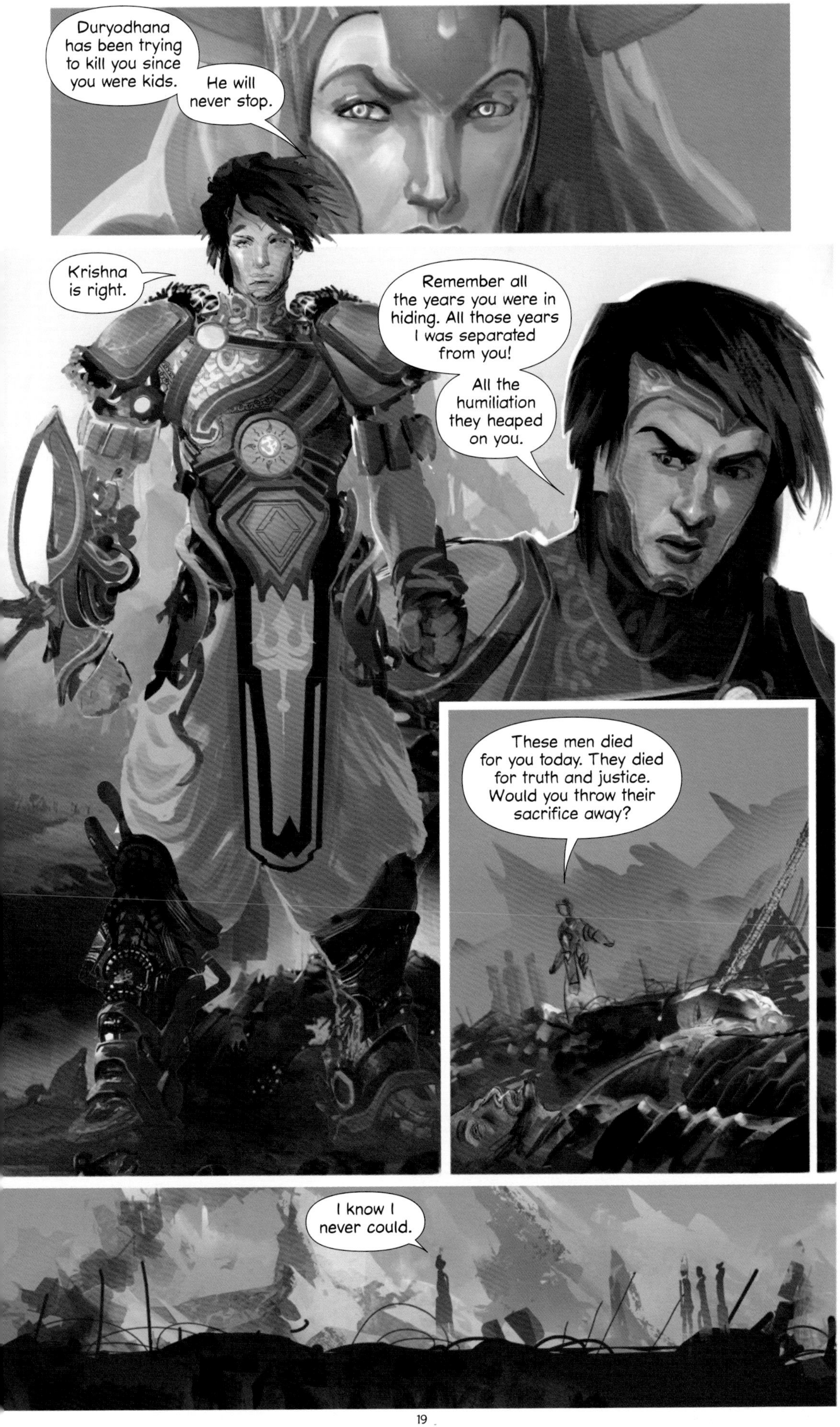

Duryodhana has been trying to kill you since you were kids.
He will never stop.
Krishna is right.
Remember all the years you were in hiding. All those years I was separated from you!
All the humiliation they heaped on you.
These men died for you today. They died for truth and justice. Would you throw their sacrifice away?
I know I never could.

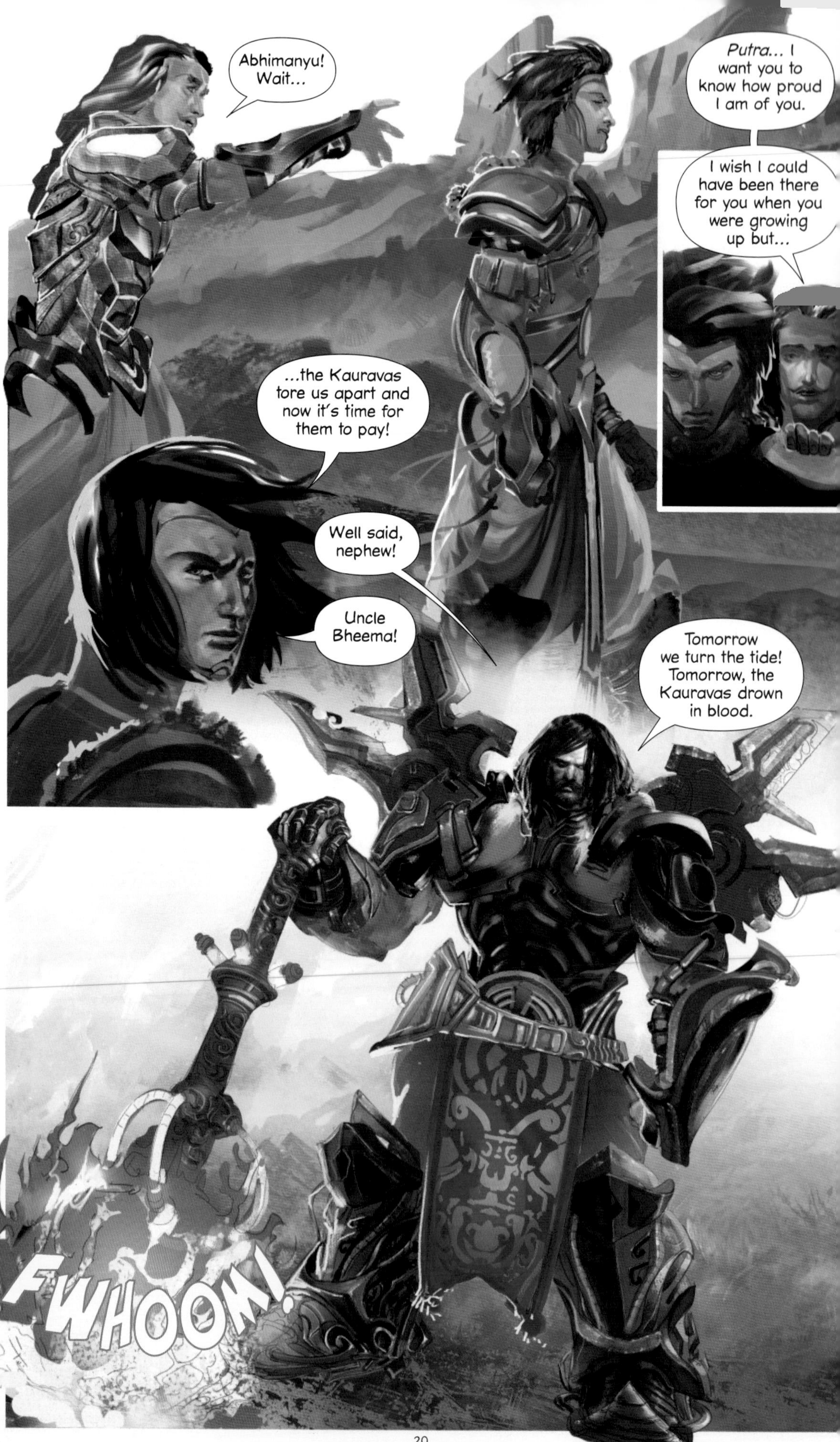
Abhimanyu! Wait...
Putra... I want you to know how proud I am of you.
I wish I could have been there for you when you were growing up but...
...the Kauravas tore us apart and now it's time for them to pay!
Well said, nephew!
Uncle Bheema!
Tomorrow we turn the tide! Tomorrow, the Kauravas drown in blood.
FWHOOM!

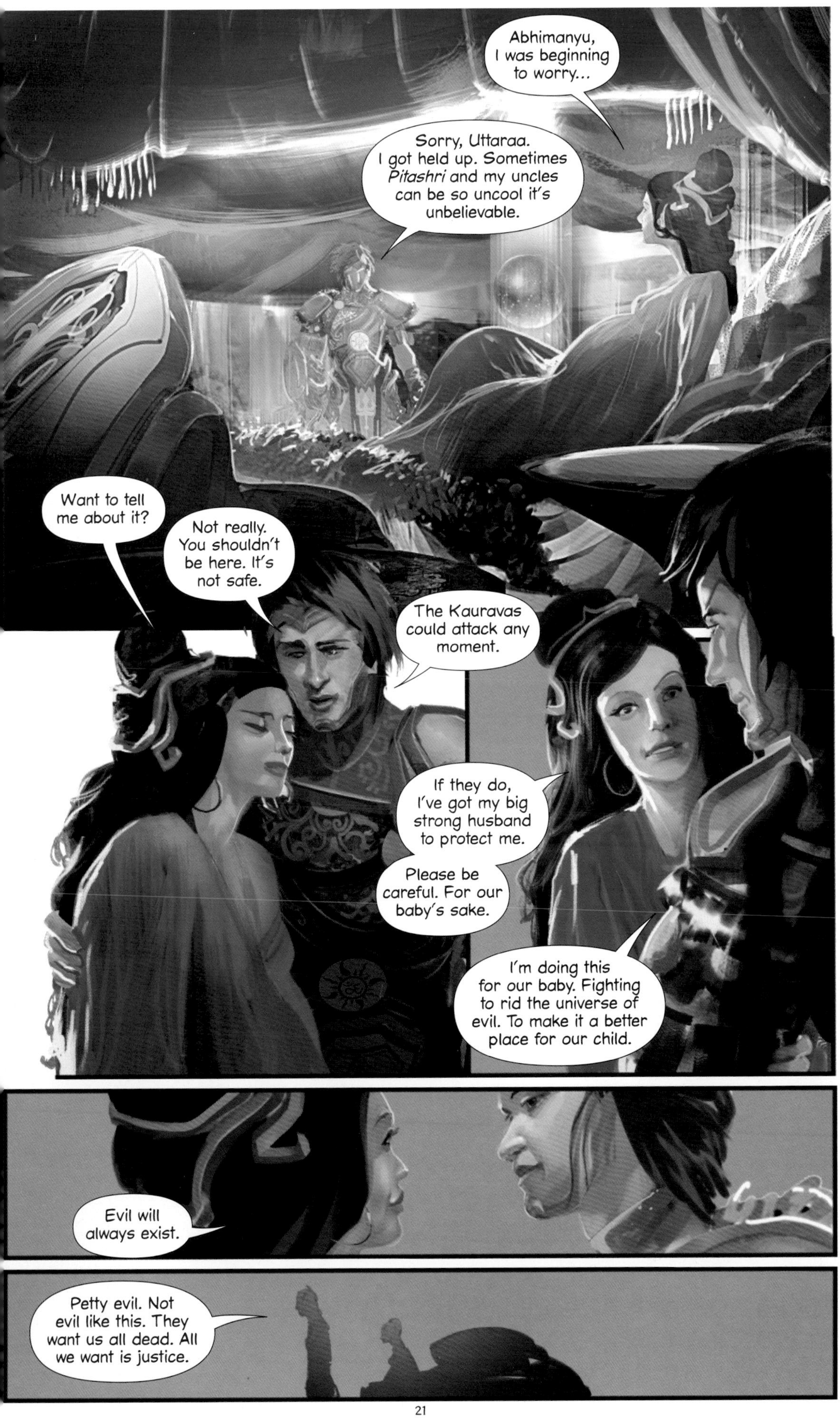
Abhimanyu, I was beginning to worry...
Sorry, Uttaraa. I got held up. Sometimes *Pitashri* and my uncles can be so uncool it's unbelievable.
Want to tell me about it?
Not really. You shouldn't be here. It's not safe.
The Kauravas could attack any moment.
If they do, I've got my big strong husband to protect me.
Please be careful. For our baby's sake.
I'm doing this for our baby. Fighting to rid the universe of evil. To make it a better place for our child.
Evil will always exist.
Petty evil. Not evil like this. They want us all dead. All we want is justice.

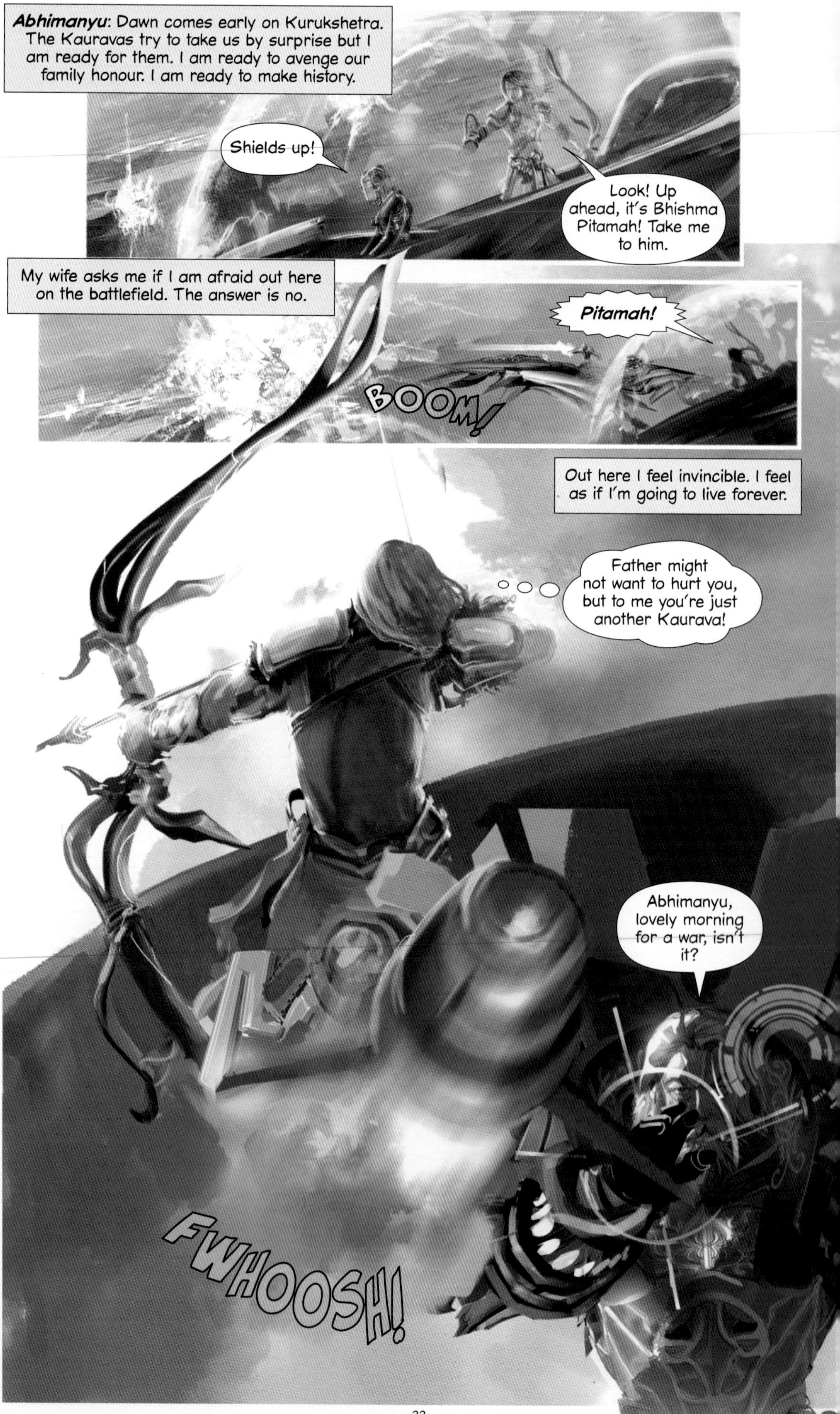

Abhimanyu: Dawn comes early on Kurukshetra. The Kauravas try to take us by surprise but I am ready for them. I am ready to avenge our family honour. I am ready to make history.
Shields up!
Look! Up ahead, it's Bhishma Pitamah! Take me to him.
My wife asks me if I am afraid out here on the battlefield. The answer is no.
Pitamah!
BOOM!
Out here I feel invincible. I feel as if I'm going to live forever.
Father might not want to hurt you, but to me you're just another Kaurava!
Abhimanyu, lovely morning for a war, isn't it?
FWHOOSH!

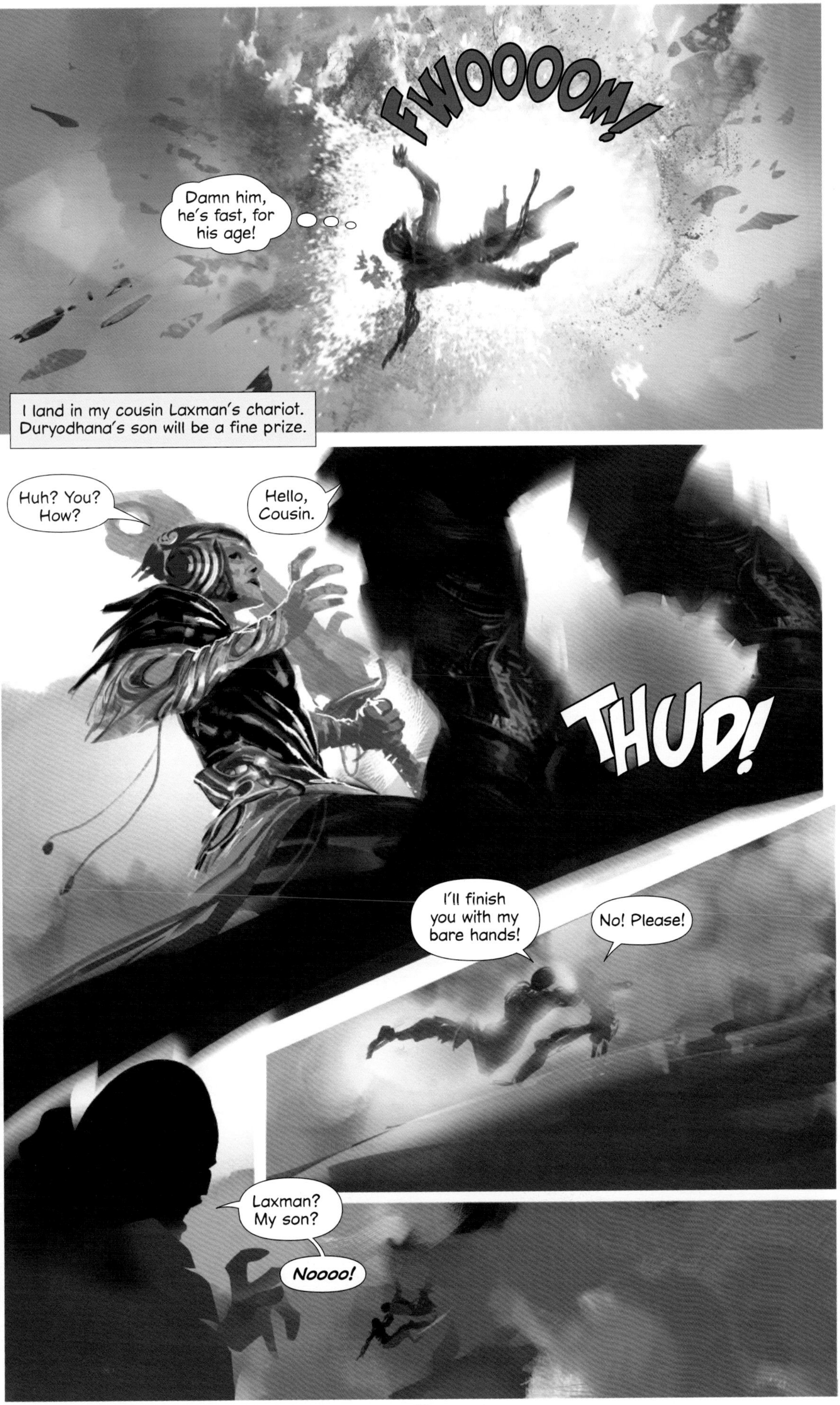
FWOOOOM!
Damn him, he's fast, for his age!
I land in my cousin Laxman's chariot. Duryodhana's son will be a fine prize.
Huh? You? How?
Hello, Cousin.
THUD!
I'll finish you with my bare hands!
No! Please!
Laxman? My son?
Noooo!

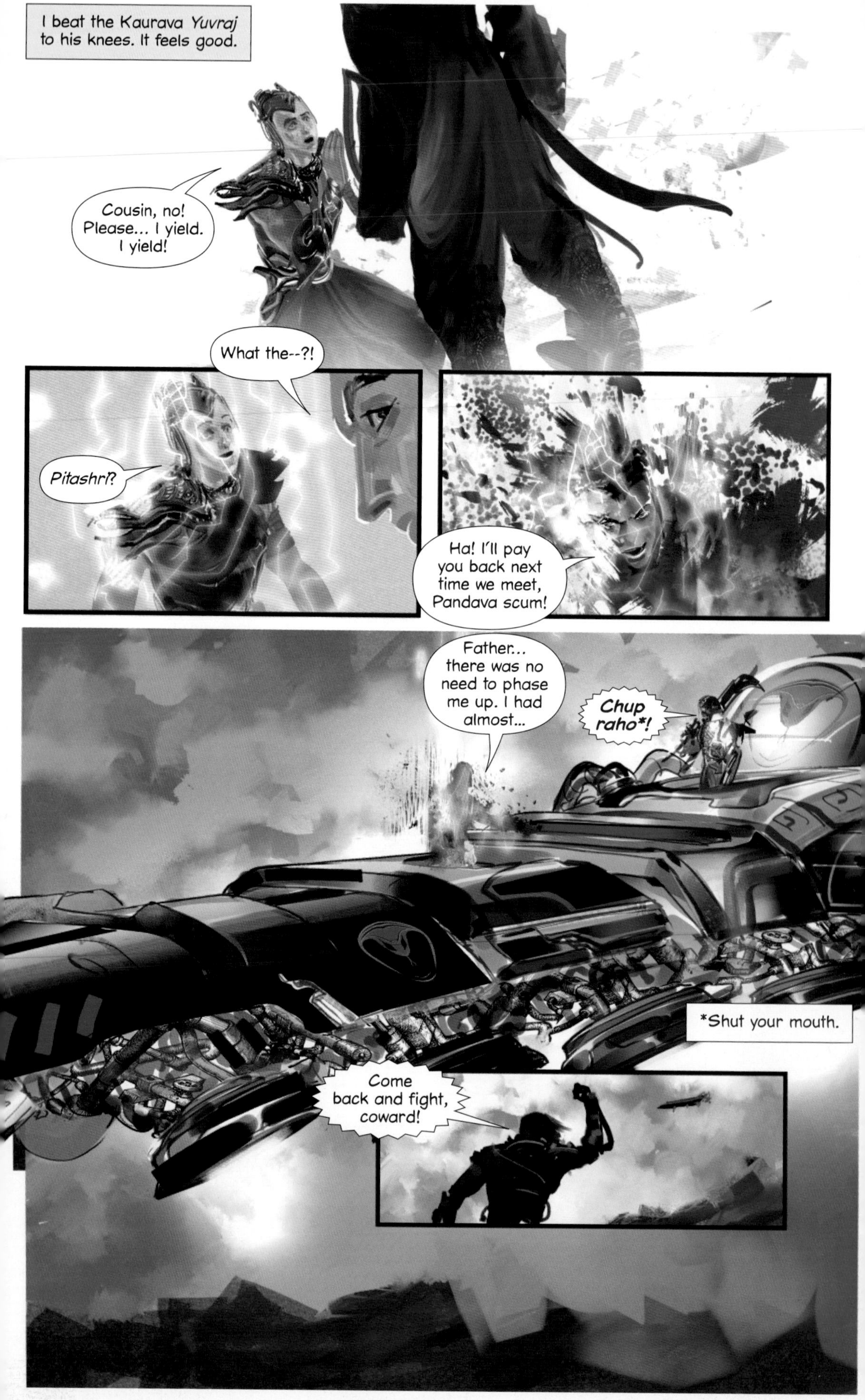
I beat the Kaurava *Yuvraj* to his knees. It feels good.
Cousin, no! Please... I yield. I yield!
What the--?!
Pitashri?
Ha! I'll pay you back next time we meet, Pandava scum!
Father... there was no need to phase me up. I had almost...
Chup raho*!
*Shut your mouth.
Come back and fight, coward!

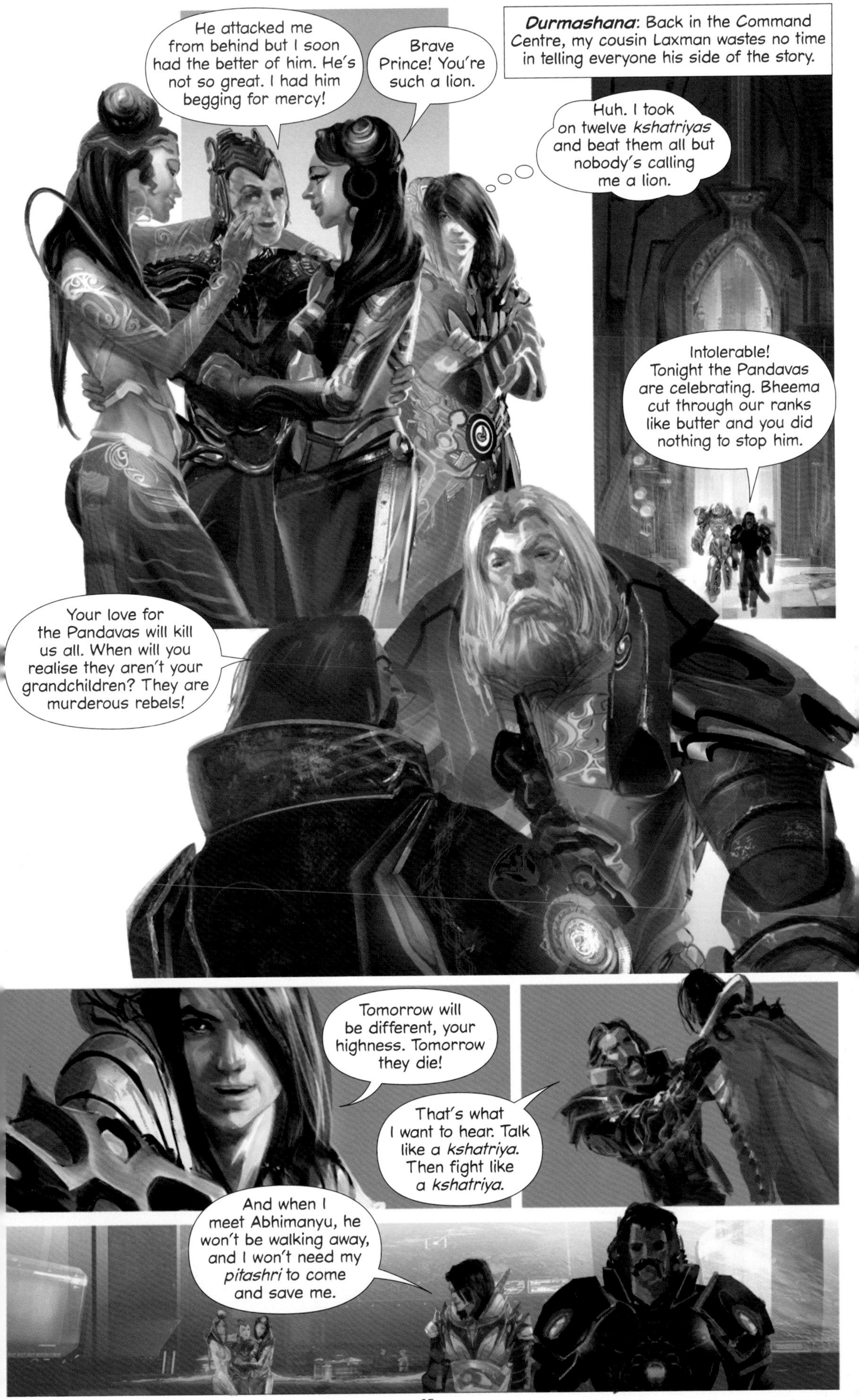
Durmashana: Back in the Command Centre, my cousin Laxman wastes no time in telling everyone his side of the story.
He attacked me from behind but I soon had the better of him. He's not so great. I had him begging for mercy!
Brave Prince! You're such a lion.
Huh. I took on twelve kshatriyas and beat them all but nobody's calling me a lion.
Intolerable! Tonight the Pandavas are celebrating. Bheema cut through our ranks like butter and you did nothing to stop him.
Your love for the Pandavas will kill us all. When will you realise they aren't your grandchildren? They are murderous rebels!
Tomorrow will be different, your highness. Tomorrow they die!
That's what I want to hear. Talk like a kshatriya. Then fight like a kshatriya.
And when I meet Abhimanyu, he won't be walking away, and I won't need my pitashri to come and save me.

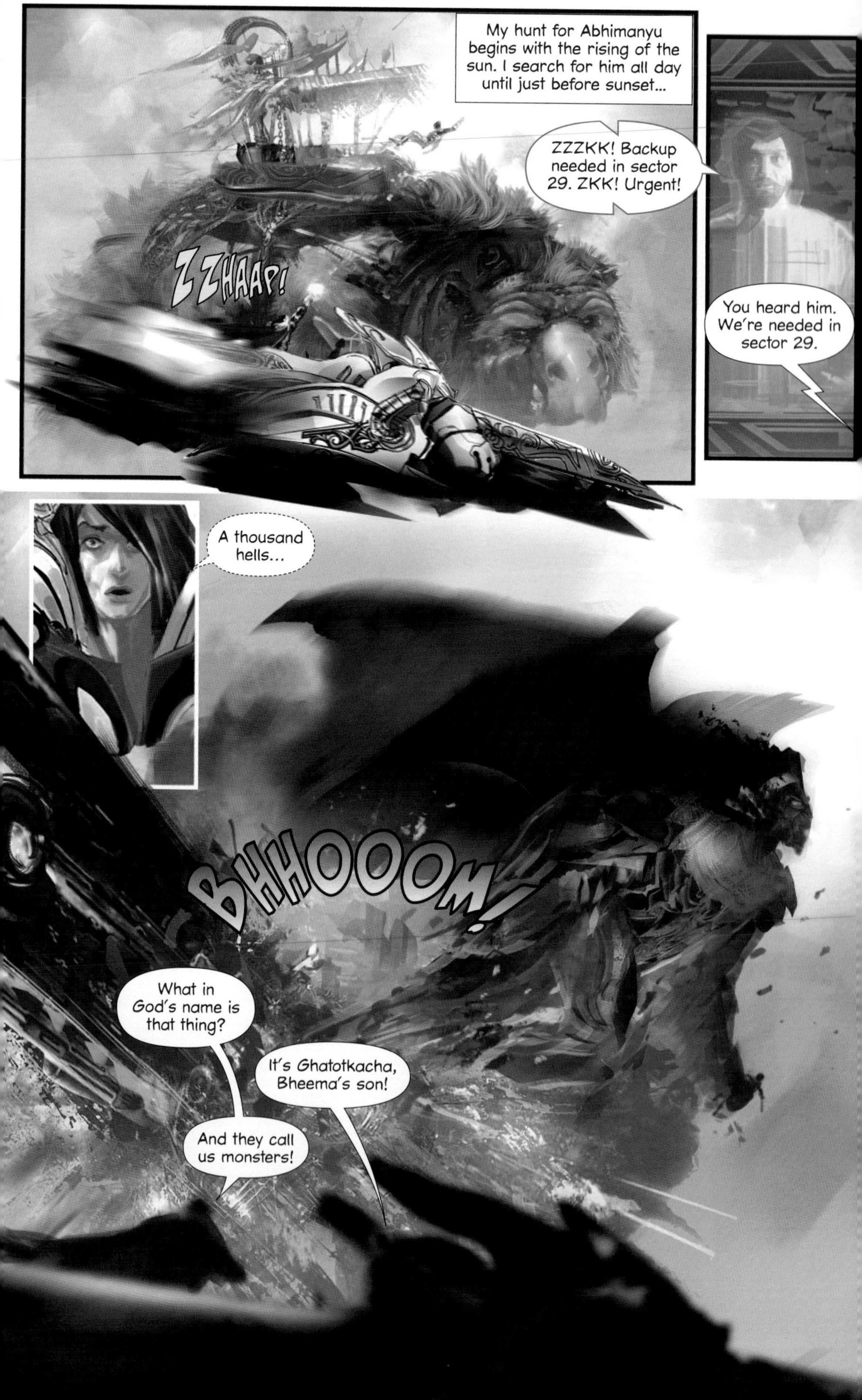

My hunt for Abhimanyu begins with the rising of the sun. I search for him all day until just before sunset...
ZZZKK! Backup needed in sector 29. ZKK! Urgent!
Z ZHAAP!
You heard him. We're needed in sector 29.
A thousand hells...
BHHOOOM!
What in God's name is that thing?
It's Ghatotkacha, Bheema's son!
And they call us monsters!

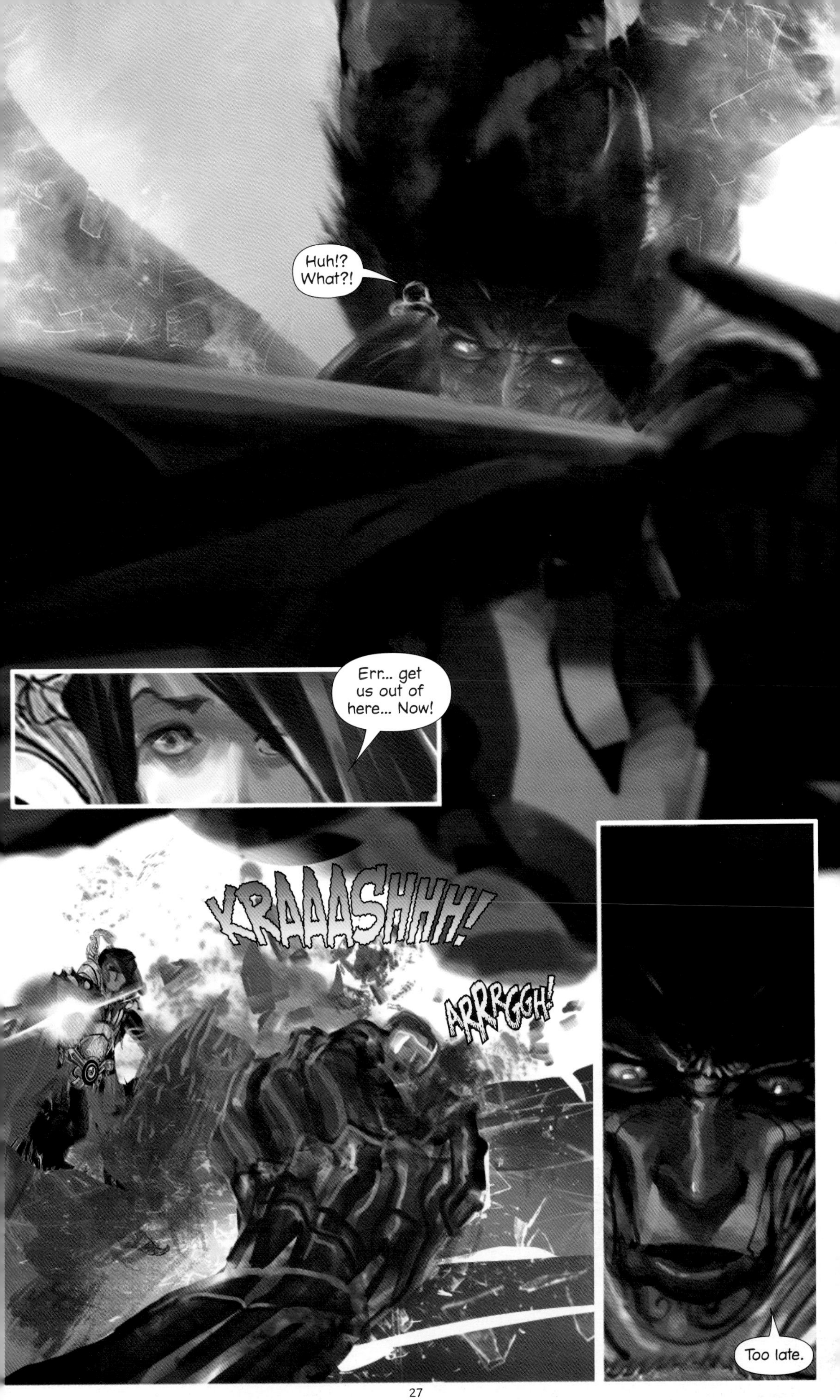
Huh!? What?!
Err... get us out of here... Now!
KRAAASHHH!
ARRRGGH!
Too late.

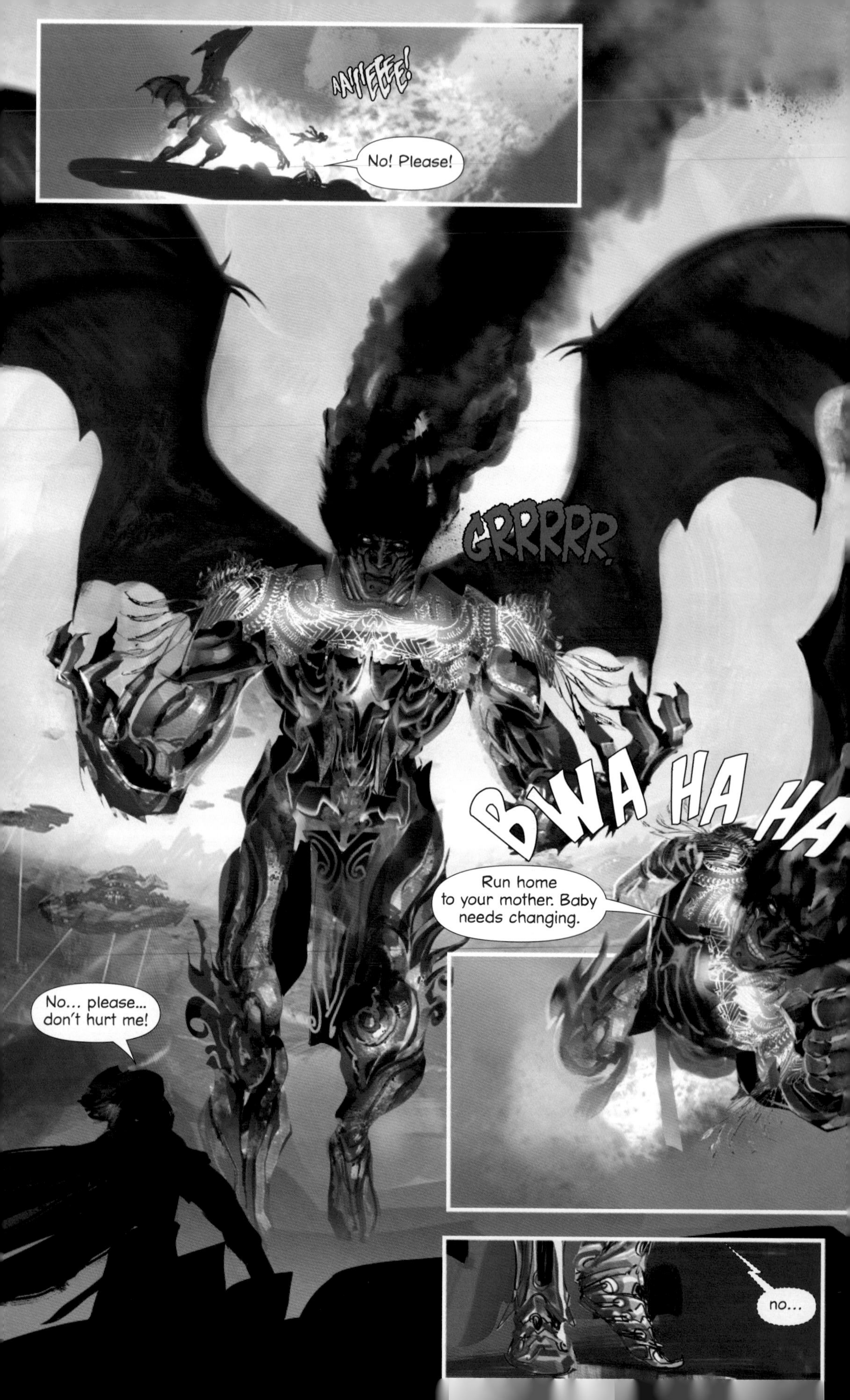
AAIIIEEEE!
No! Please!
GRRRRR.
BWA HA HA
Run home to your mother. Baby needs changing.
No... please... don't hurt me!
no...

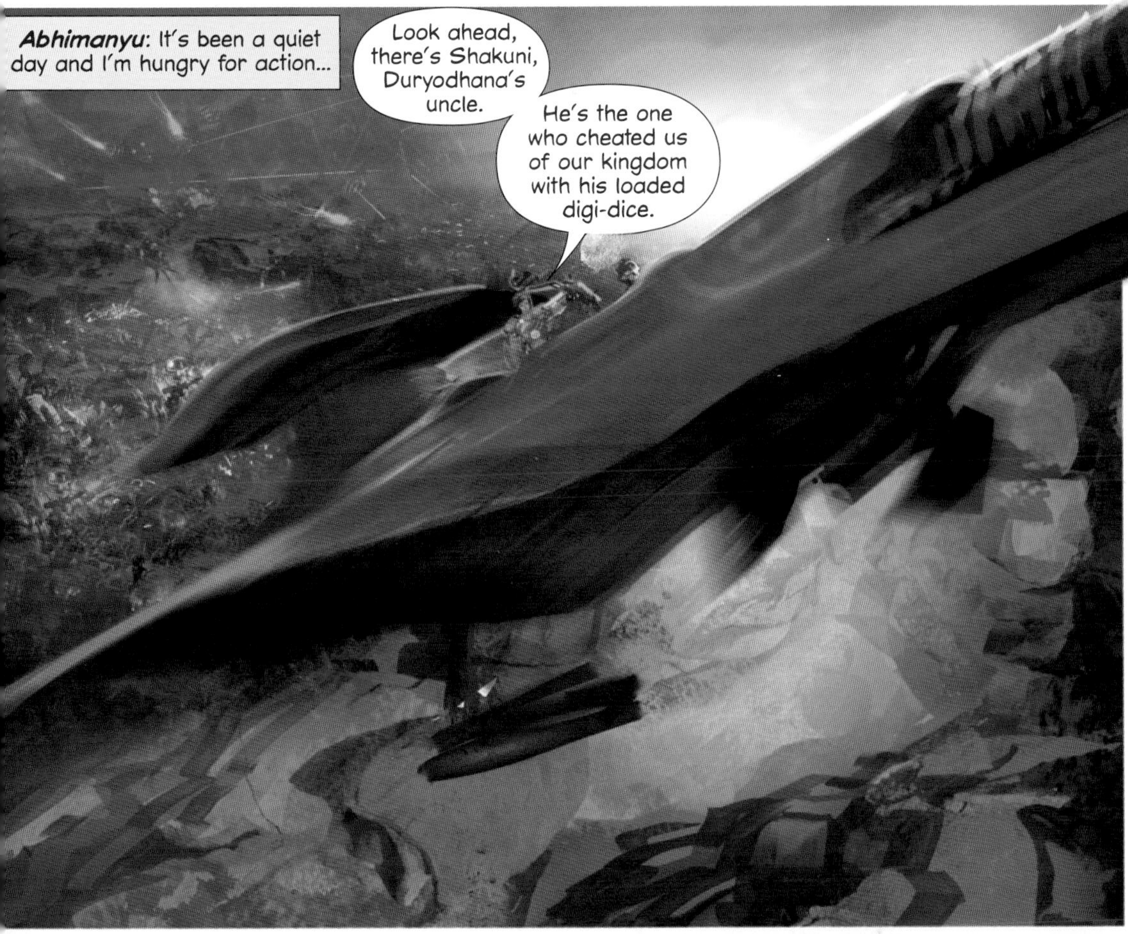
Abhimanyu: It's been a quiet day and I'm hungry for action...
Look ahead, there's Shakuni, Duryodhana's uncle.
He's the one who cheated us of our kingdom with his loaded digi-dice.

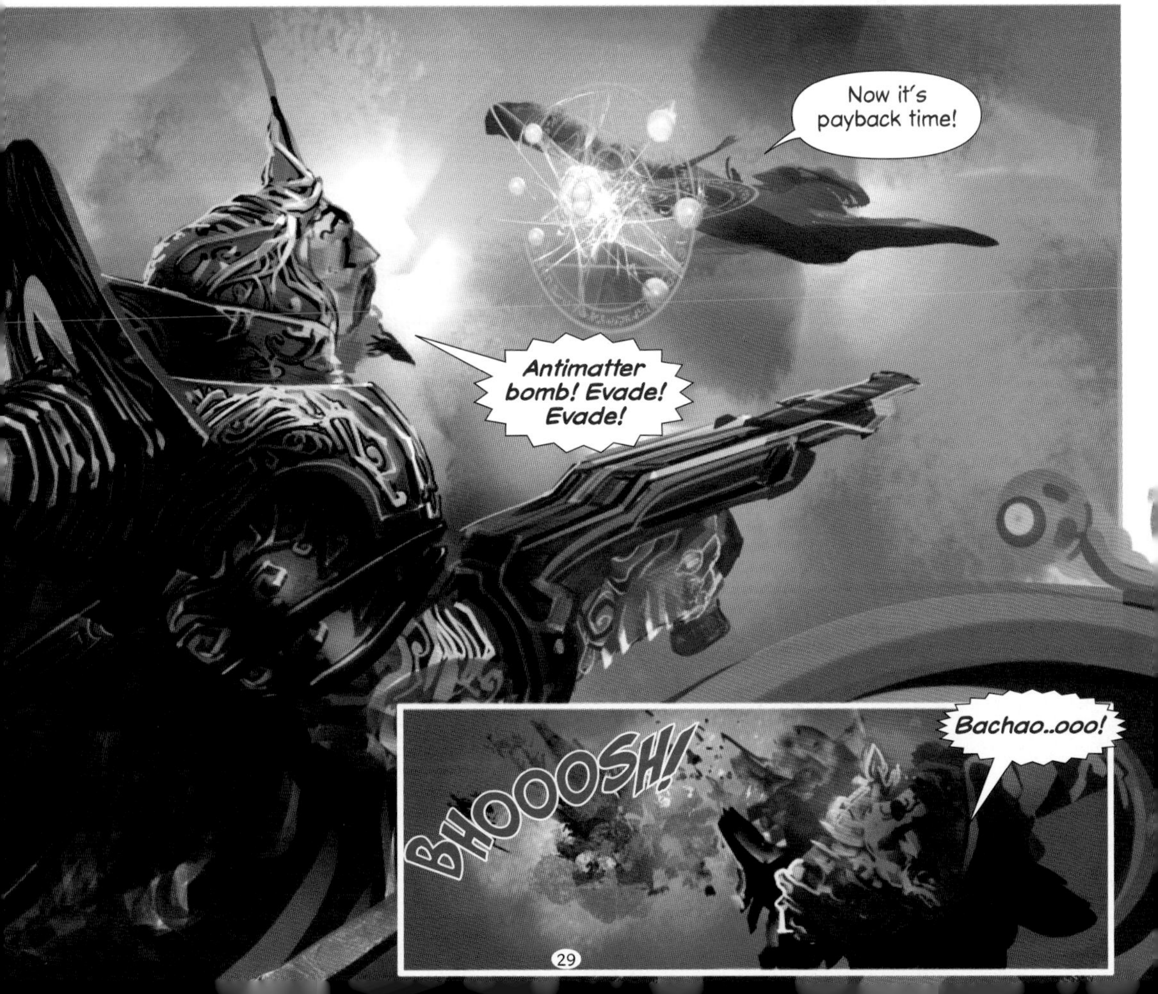
Now it's payback time!
Antimatter bomb! Evade! Evade!
BHOOOSH!
Bachao..ooo!

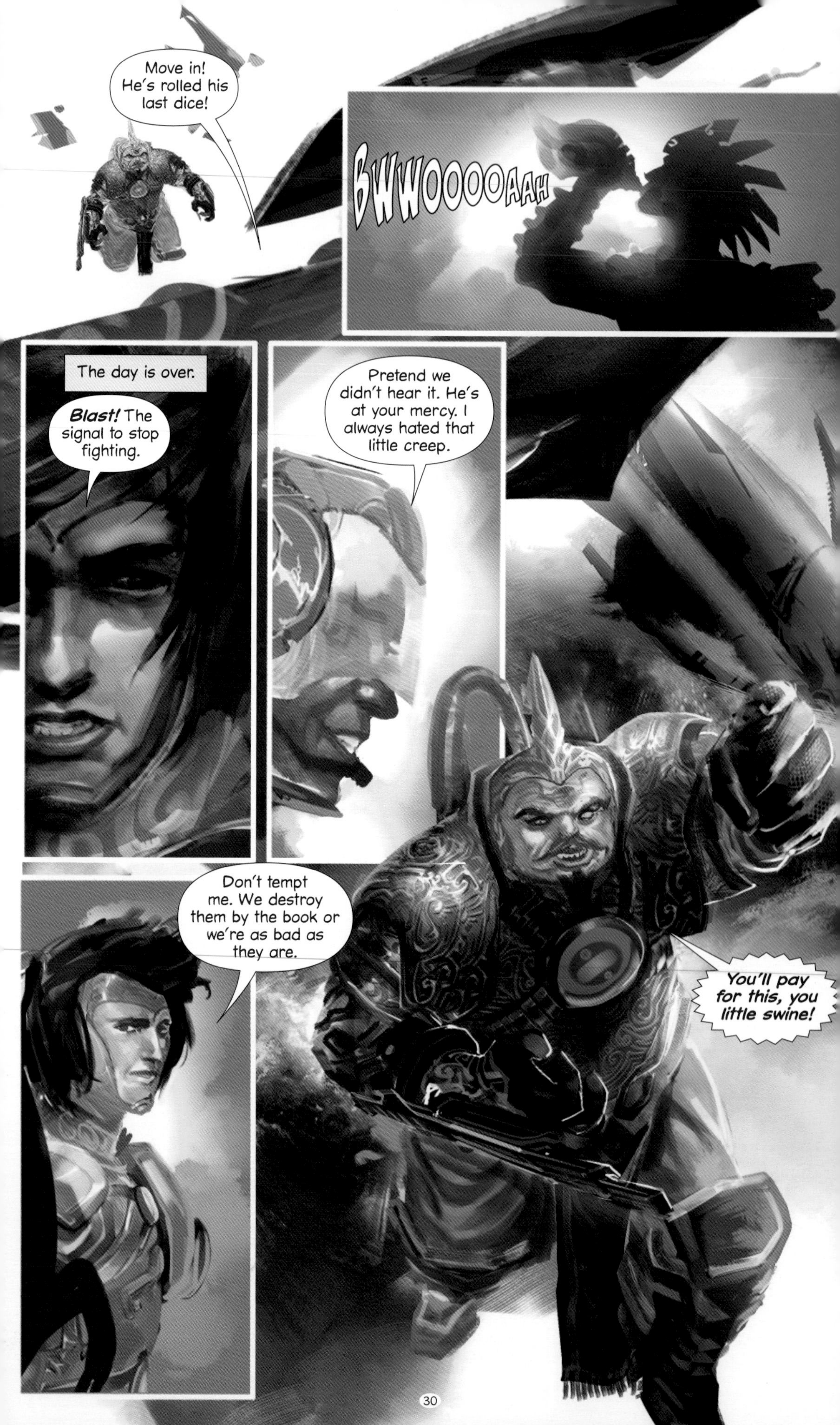
Move in! He's rolled his last dice!
BWWOOOOAAH
The day is over.
Blast! The signal to stop fighting.
Pretend we didn't hear it. He's at your mercy. I always hated that little creep.
Don't tempt me. We destroy them by the book or we're as bad as they are.
You'll pay for this, you little swine!

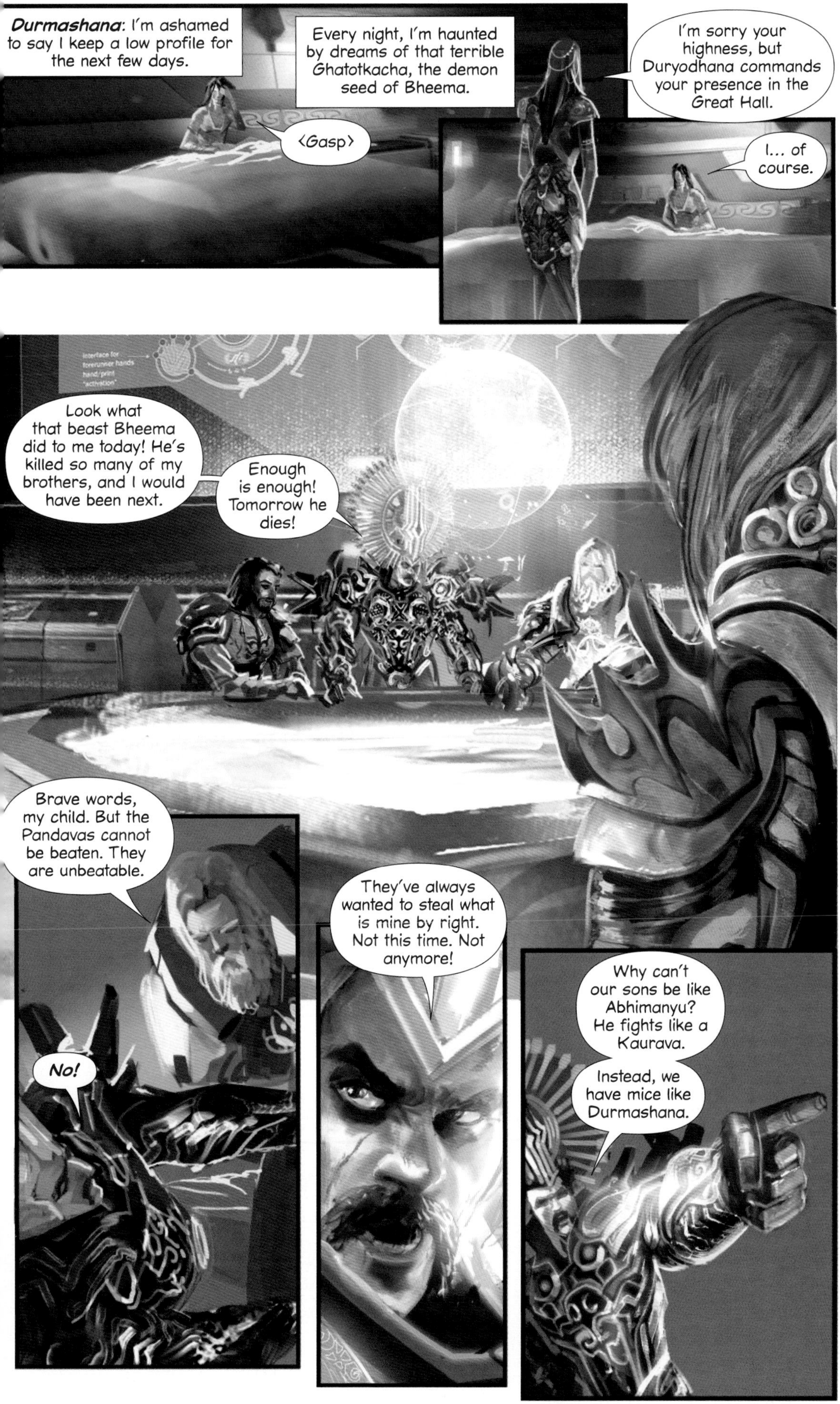

Durmashana: I'm ashamed to say I keep a low profile for the next few days.
Every night, I'm haunted by dreams of that terrible Ghatotkacha, the demon seed of Bheema.
<Gasp>
I'm sorry your highness, but Duryodhana commands your presence in the Great Hall.
I... of course.
Look what that beast Bheema did to me today! He's killed so many of my brothers, and I would have been next.
Enough is enough! Tomorrow he dies!
Brave words, my child. But the Pandavas cannot be beaten. They are unbeatable.
No!
They've always wanted to steal what is mine by right. Not this time. Not anymore!
Why can't our sons be like Abhimanyu? He fights like a Kaurava.
Instead, we have mice like Durmashana.

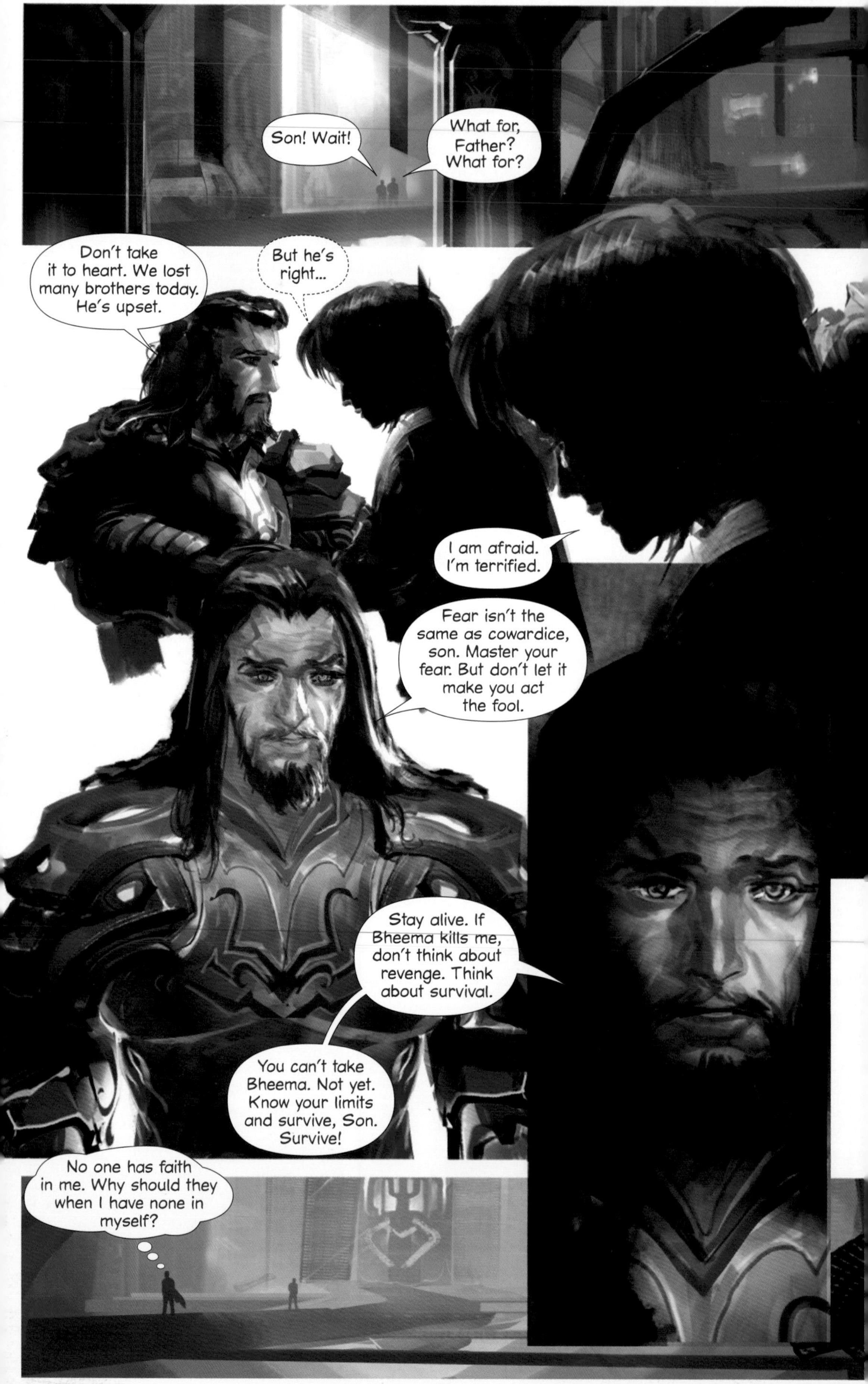
Son! Wait!
What for, Father? What for?
Don't take it to heart. We lost many brothers today. He's upset.
But he's right...
I am afraid. I'm terrified.
Fear isn't the same as cowardice, son. Master your fear. But don't let it make you act the fool.
Stay alive. If Bheema kills me, don't think about revenge. Think about survival.
You can't take Bheema. Not yet. Know your limits and survive, Son. Survive!
No one has faith in me. Why should they when I have none in myself?

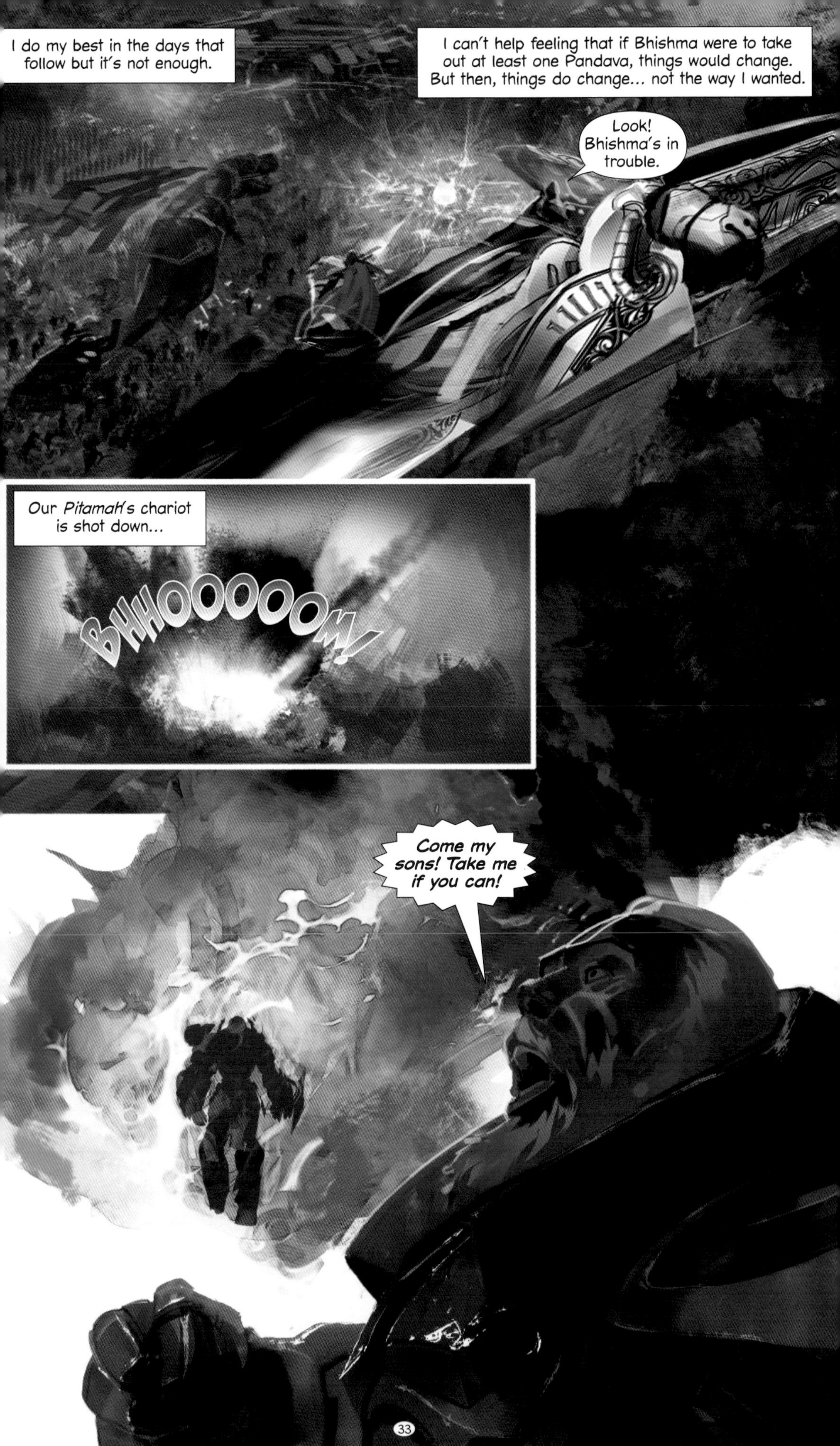

I do my best in the days that follow but it's not enough.
I can't help feeling that if Bhishma were to take out at least one Pandava, things would change. But then, things do change... not the way I wanted.
Look! Bhishma's in trouble.
Our *Pitamah*'s chariot is shot down...
BHHOOOOOOM!
Come my sons! Take me if you can!

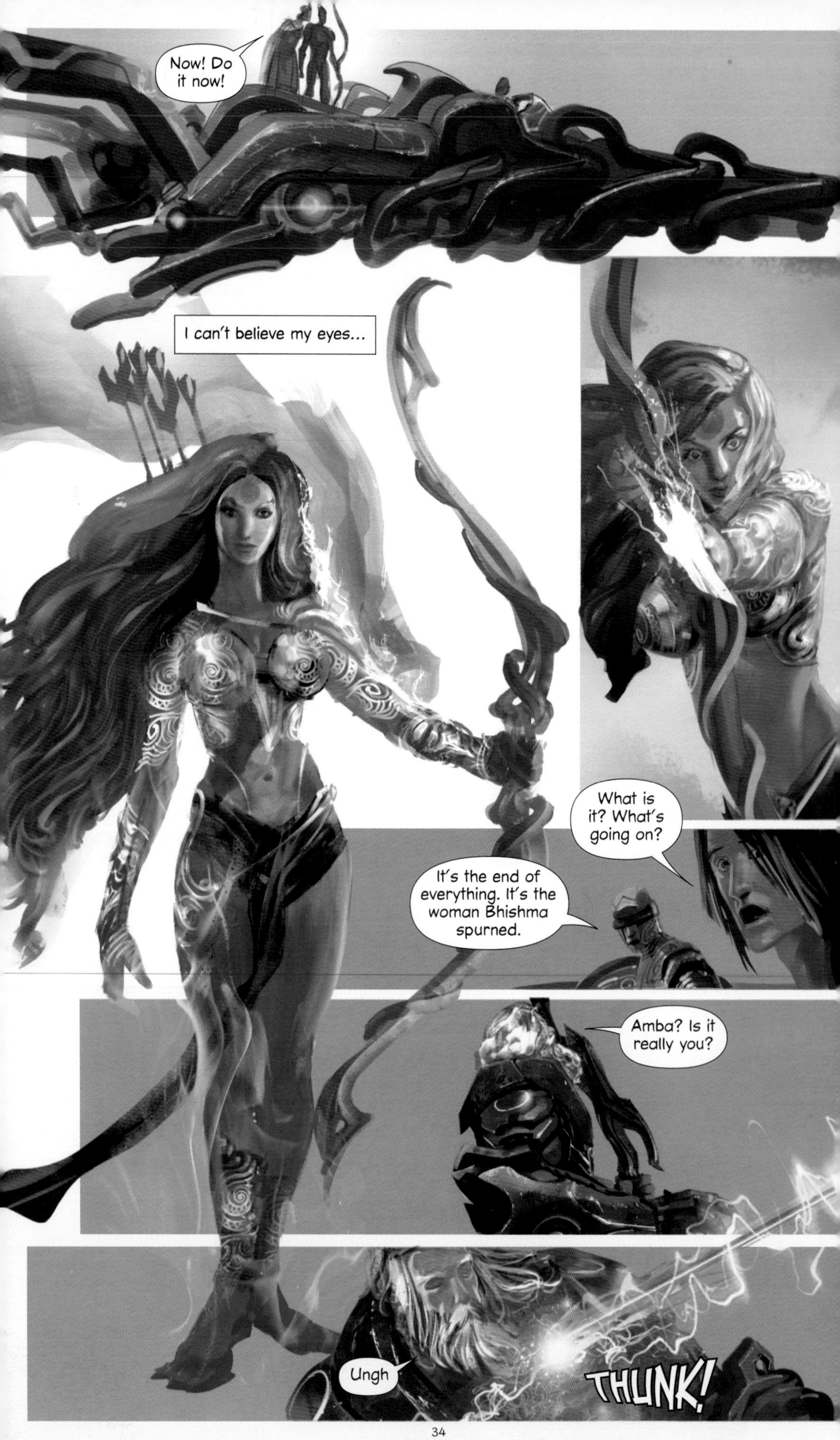

Now! Do it now!
I can't believe my eyes...
What is it? What's going on?
It's the end of everything. It's the woman Bhishma spurned.
Amba? Is it really you?
Ungh
THUNK!

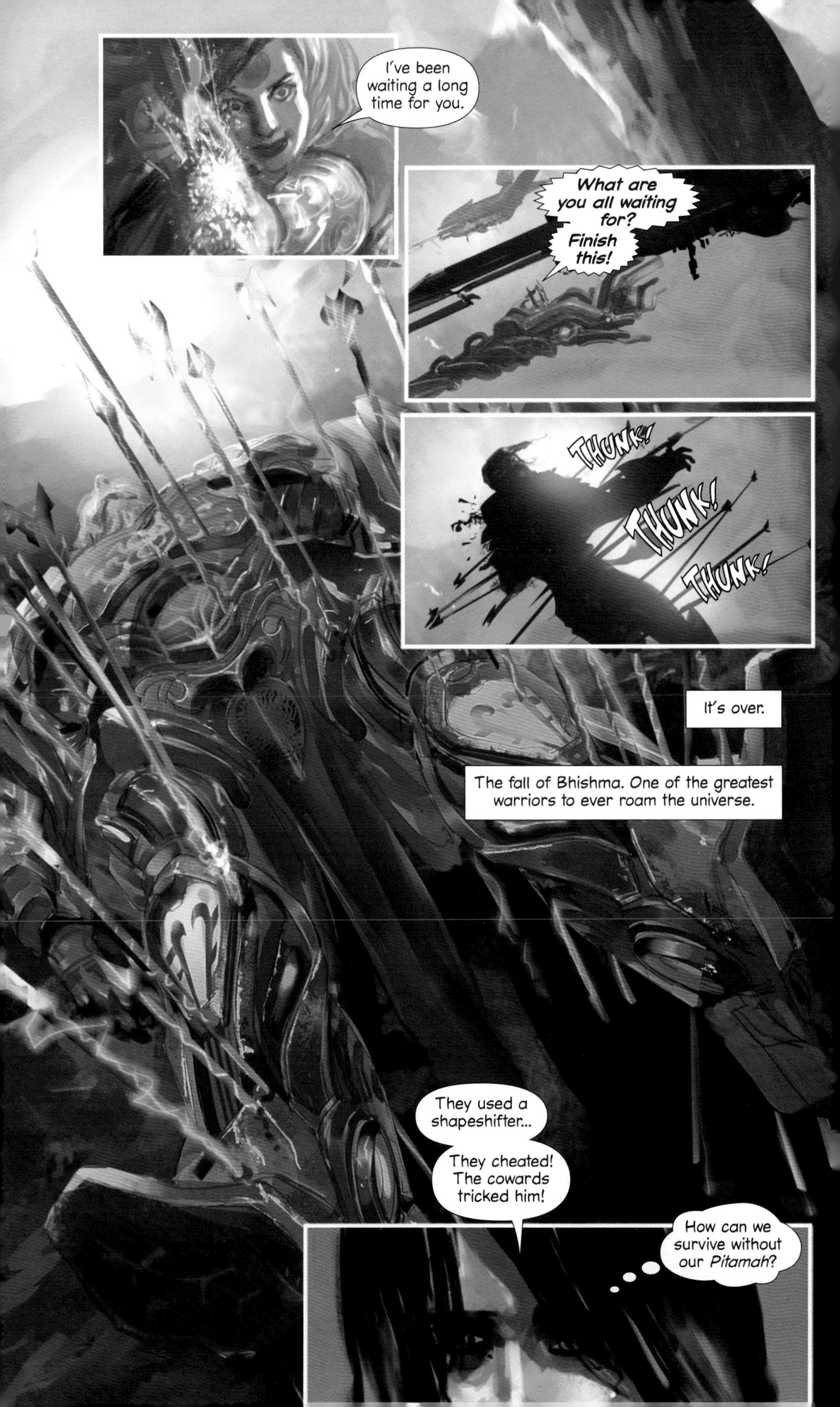

I've been waiting a long time for you.
What are you all waiting for?
Finish this!
THUNK!
THUNK!
THUNK!
It's over.
The fall of Bhishma. One of the greatest warriors to ever roam the universe.
They used a shapeshifter...
They cheated! The cowards tricked him!
How can we survive without our *Pitamah*?

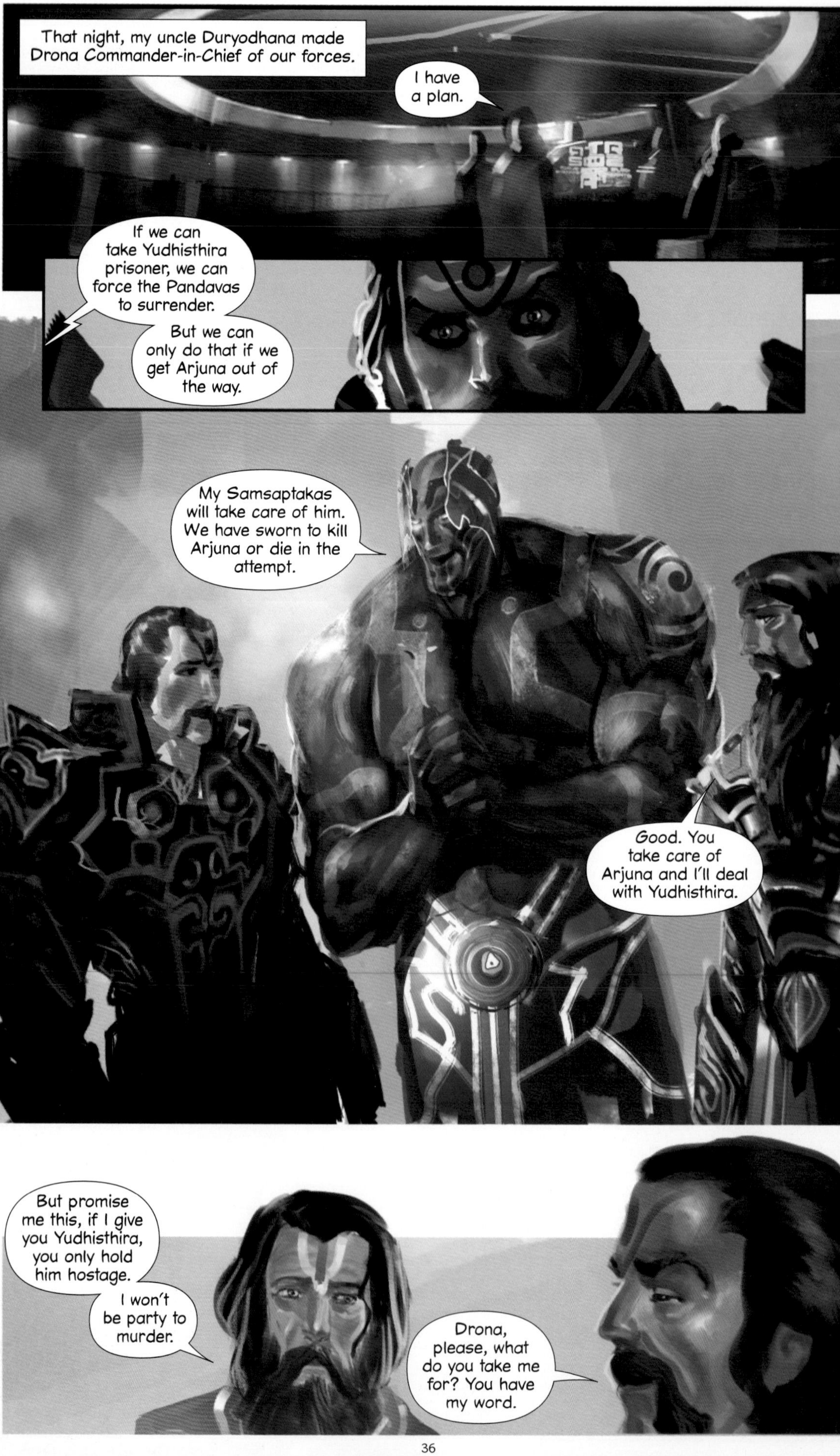

That night, my uncle Duryodhana made Drona Commander-in-Chief of our forces.
I have a plan.
If we can take Yudhisthira prisoner, we can force the Pandavas to surrender.
But we can only do that if we get Arjuna out of the way.
My Samsaptakas will take care of him. We have sworn to kill Arjuna or die in the attempt.
Good. You take care of Arjuna and I'll deal with Yudhisthira.
But promise me this, if I give you Yudhisthira, you only hold him hostage.
I won't be party to murder.
Drona, please, what do you take me for? You have my word.

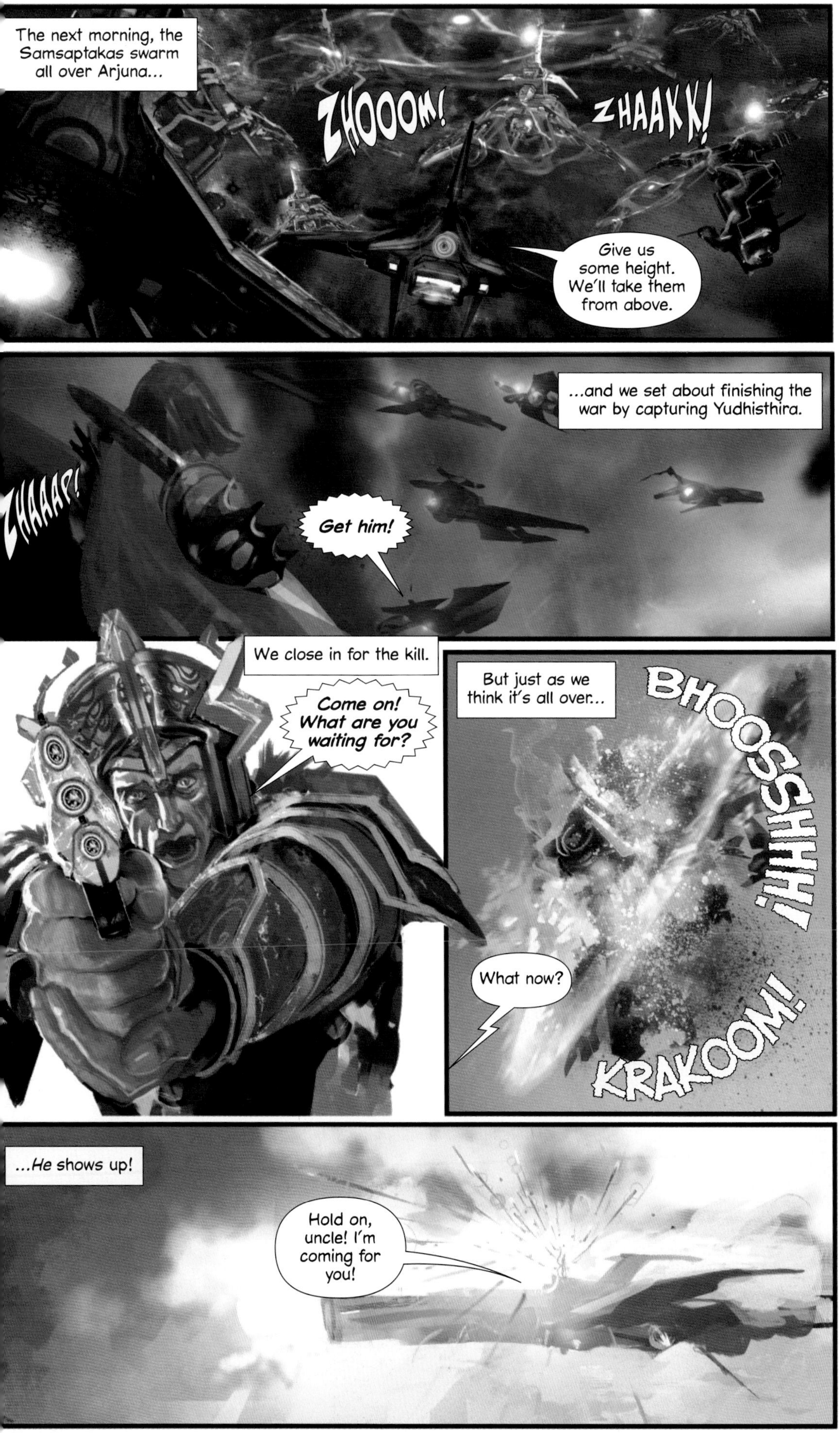
The next morning, the Samsaptakas swarm all over Arjuna...
ZHOOOM!
ZHAAKK!
Give us some height. We'll take them from above.
...and we set about finishing the war by capturing Yudhisthira.
ZHAAAP!
Get him!
We close in for the kill.
Come on! What are you waiting for?
But just as we think it's all over...
BHOOSSHHH!
What now?
KRAKOOM!
...He shows up!
Hold on, uncle! I'm coming for you!

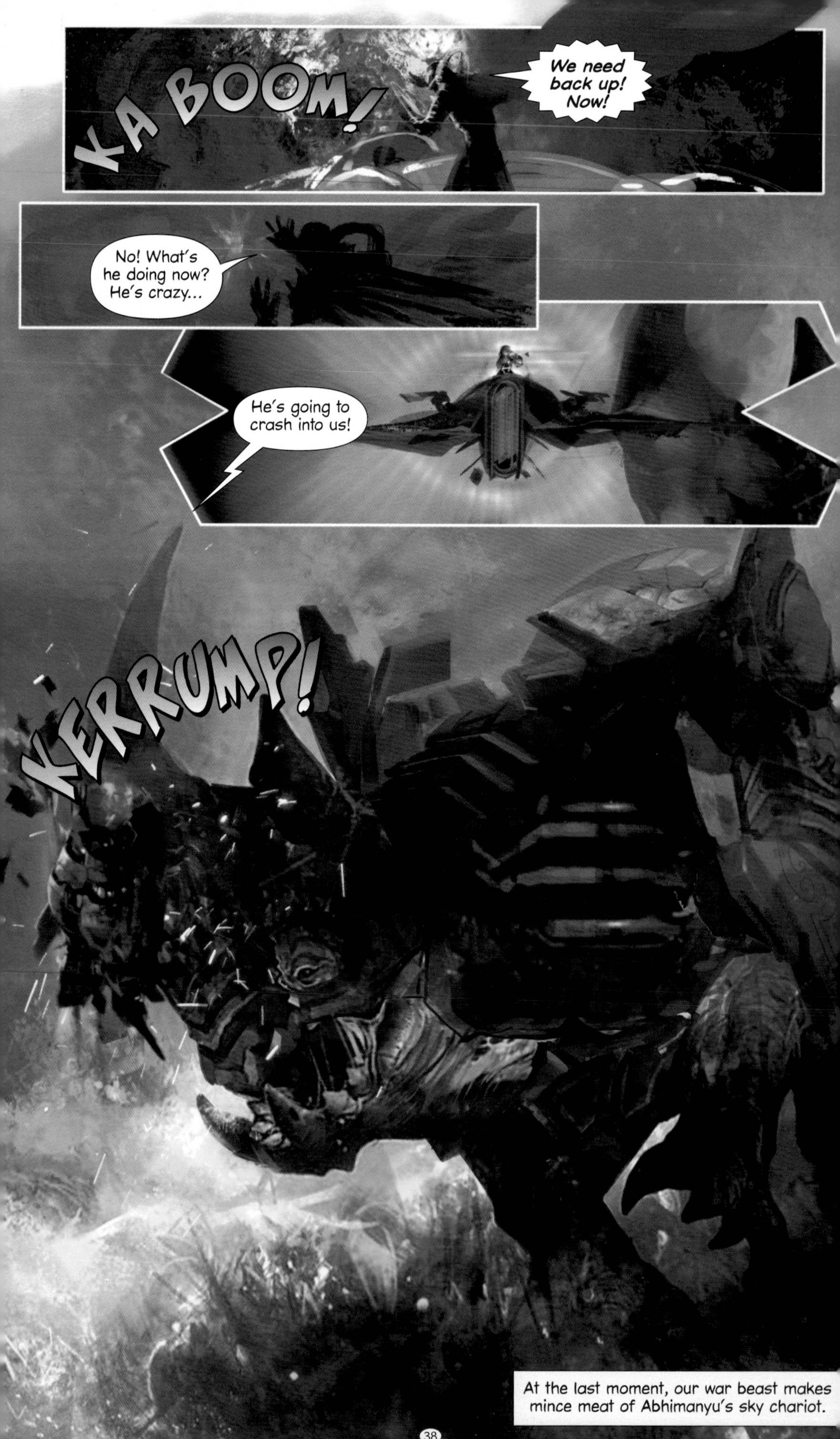
KA BOOM!
We need back up! Now!
No! What's he doing now? He's crazy...
He's going to crash into us!
KERRUMP!
At the last moment, our war beast makes mince meat of Abhimanyu's sky chariot.

Finish him off! Trample him into the mud!
THOK!
THOK!
Uncle! Run! Leave me!
Never.

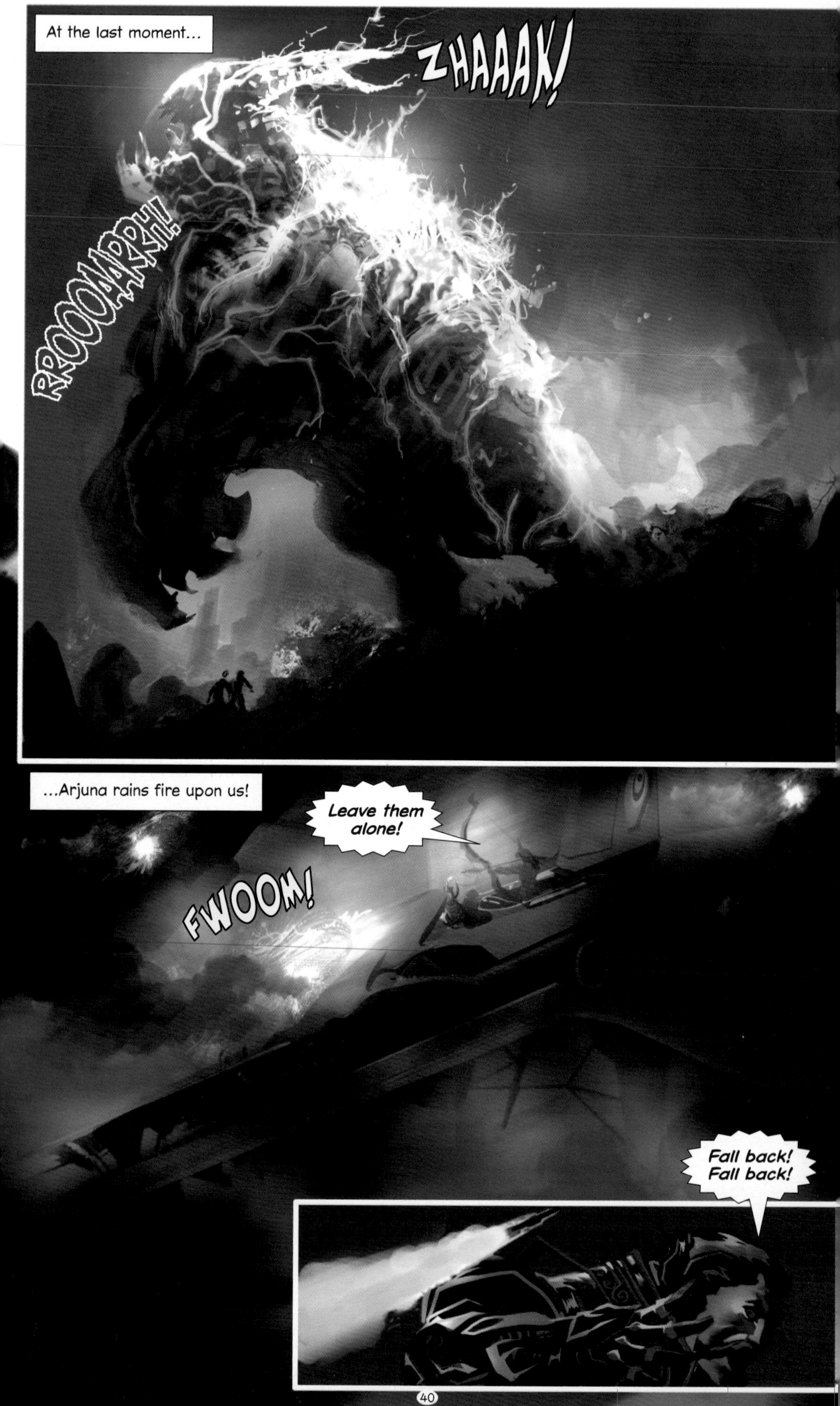
At the last moment...
ZHAAAK!
BROOOARRH!
...Arjuna rains fire upon us!
Leave them alone!
FWOOM!
Fall back! Fall back!

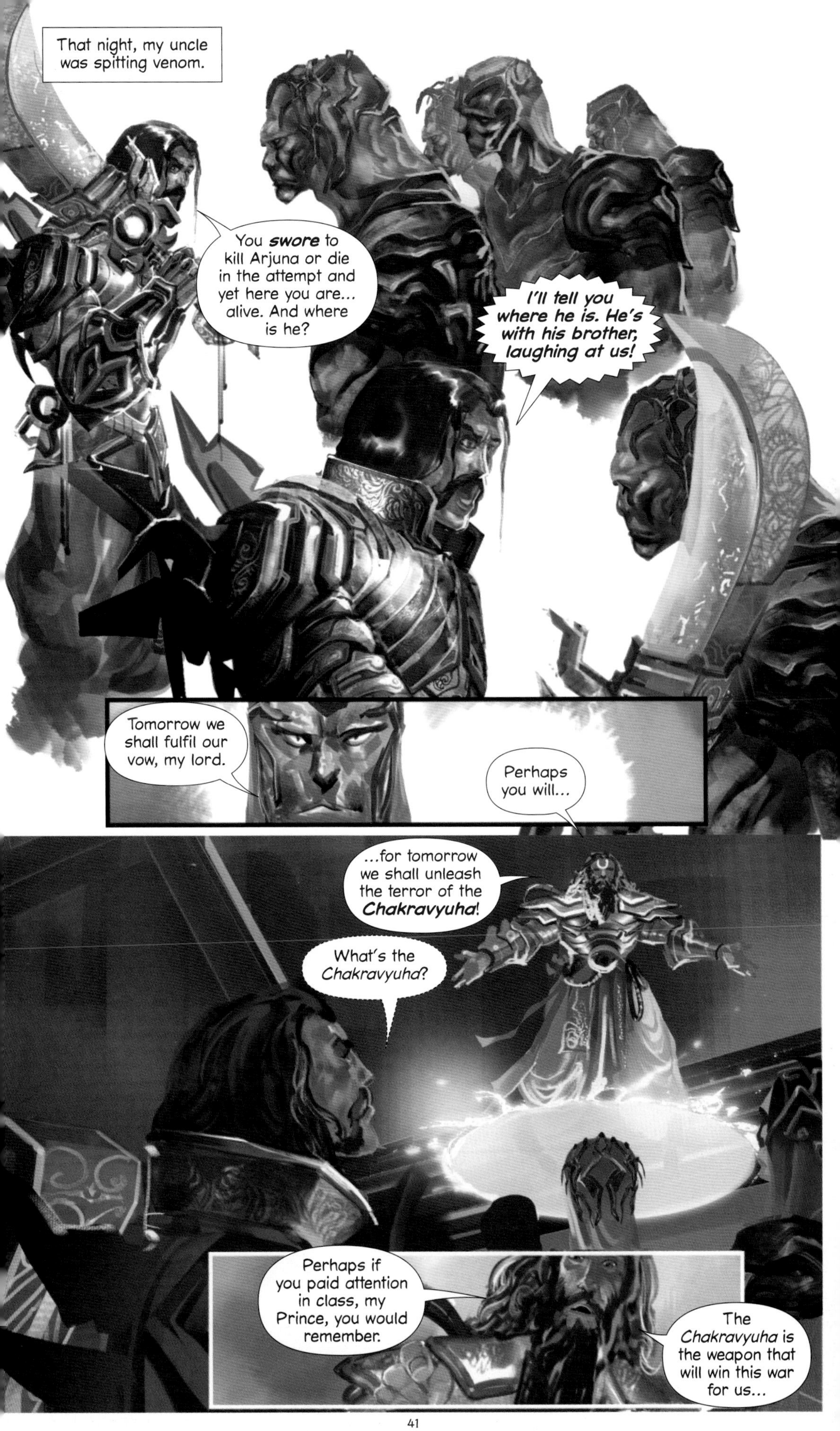
That night, my uncle was spitting venom.
You **swore** to kill Arjuna or die in the attempt and yet here you are... alive. And where is he?
I'll tell you where he is. He's with his brother, laughing at us!
Tomorrow we shall fulfil our vow, my lord.
Perhaps you will...
...for tomorrow we shall unleash the terror of the **Chakravyuha**!
What's the *Chakravyuha*?
Perhaps if you paid attention in class, my Prince, you would remember.
The *Chakravyuha* is the weapon that will win this war for us...

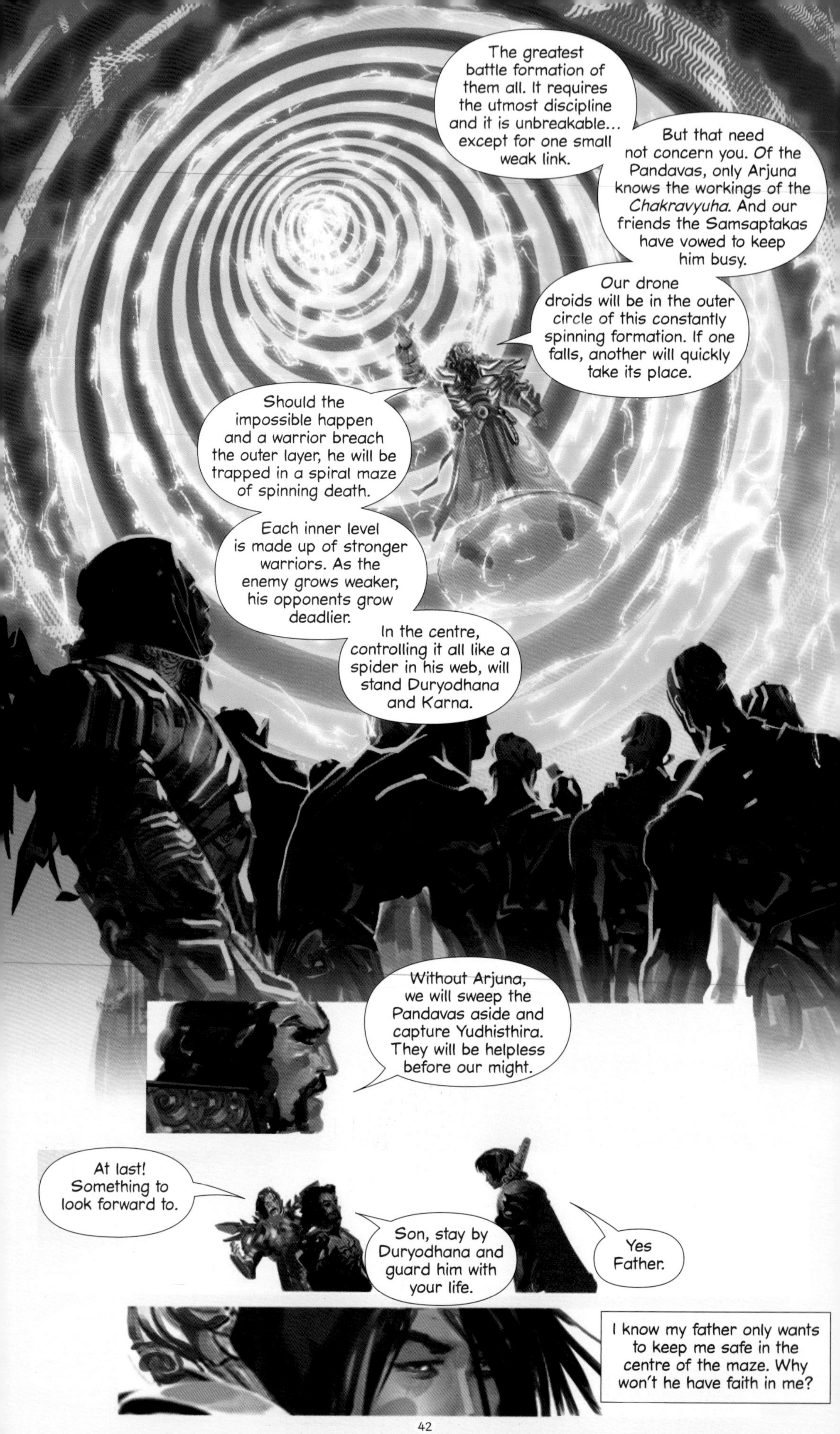
The greatest battle formation of them all. It requires the utmost discipline and it is unbreakable... except for one small weak link.
But that need not concern you. Of the Pandavas, only Arjuna knows the workings of the *Chakravyuha*. And our friends the Samsaptakas have vowed to keep him busy.
Our drone droids will be in the outer circle of this constantly spinning formation. If one falls, another will quickly take its place.
Should the impossible happen and a warrior breach the outer layer, he will be trapped in a spiral maze of spinning death.
Each inner level is made up of stronger warriors. As the enemy grows weaker, his opponents grow deadlier.
In the centre, controlling it all like a spider in his web, will stand Duryodhana and Karna.
Without Arjuna, we will sweep the Pandavas aside and capture Yudhisthira. They will be helpless before our might.
At last! Something to look forward to.
Son, stay by Duryodhana and guard him with your life.
Yes Father.
I know my father only wants to keep me safe in the centre of the maze. Why won't he have faith in me?

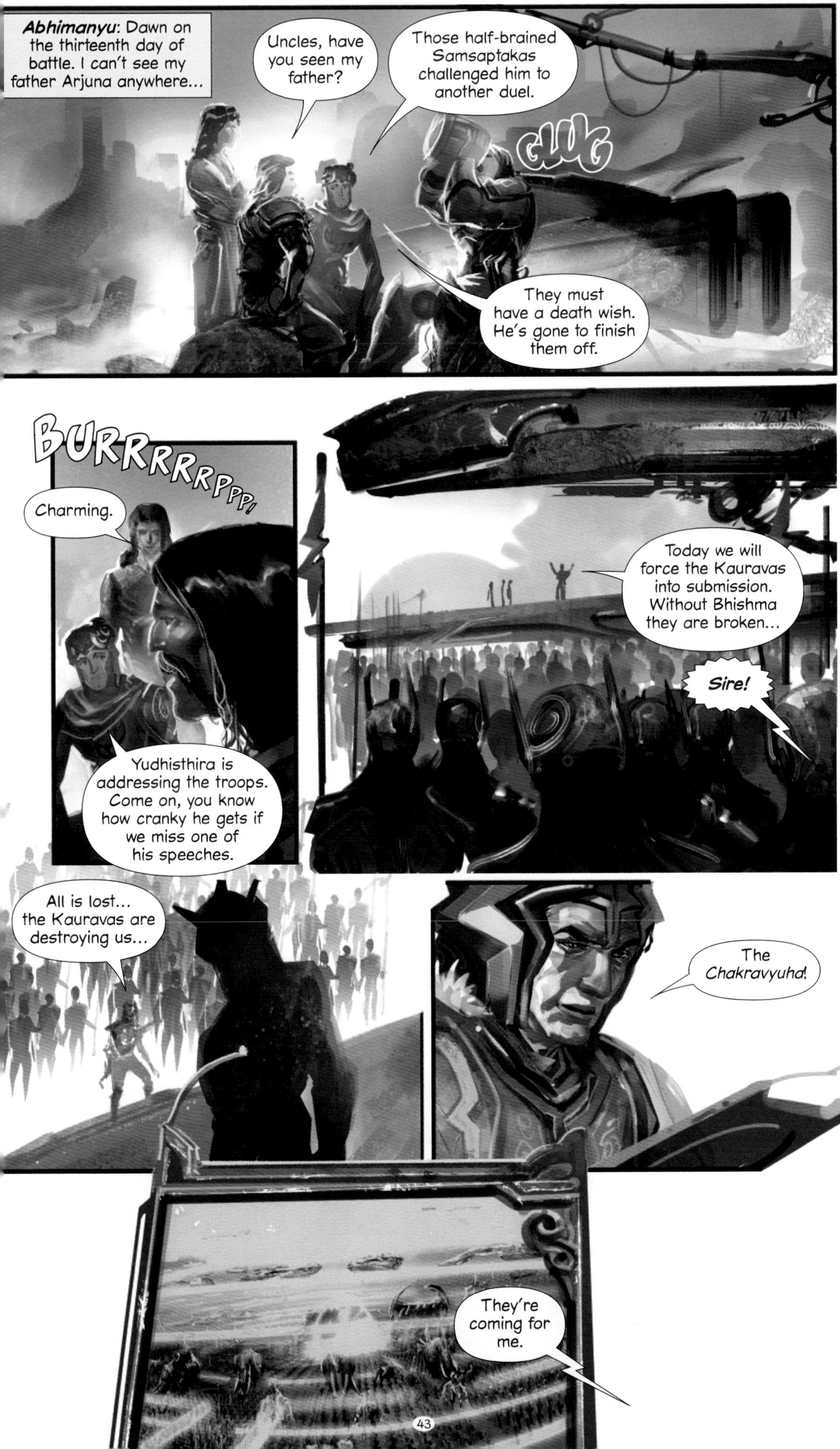
Abhimanyu: Dawn on the thirteenth day of battle. I can't see my father Arjuna anywhere...
Uncles, have you seen my father?
Those half-brained Samsaptakas challenged him to another duel.
GLUG
They must have a death wish. He's gone to finish them off.
BURRRRRPPP!
Charming.
Yudhisthira is addressing the troops. Come on, you know how cranky he gets if we miss one of his speeches.
Today we will force the Kauravas into submission. Without Bhishma they are broken...
Sire!
All is lost... the Kauravas are destroying us...
The Chakravyuha!
They're coming for me.

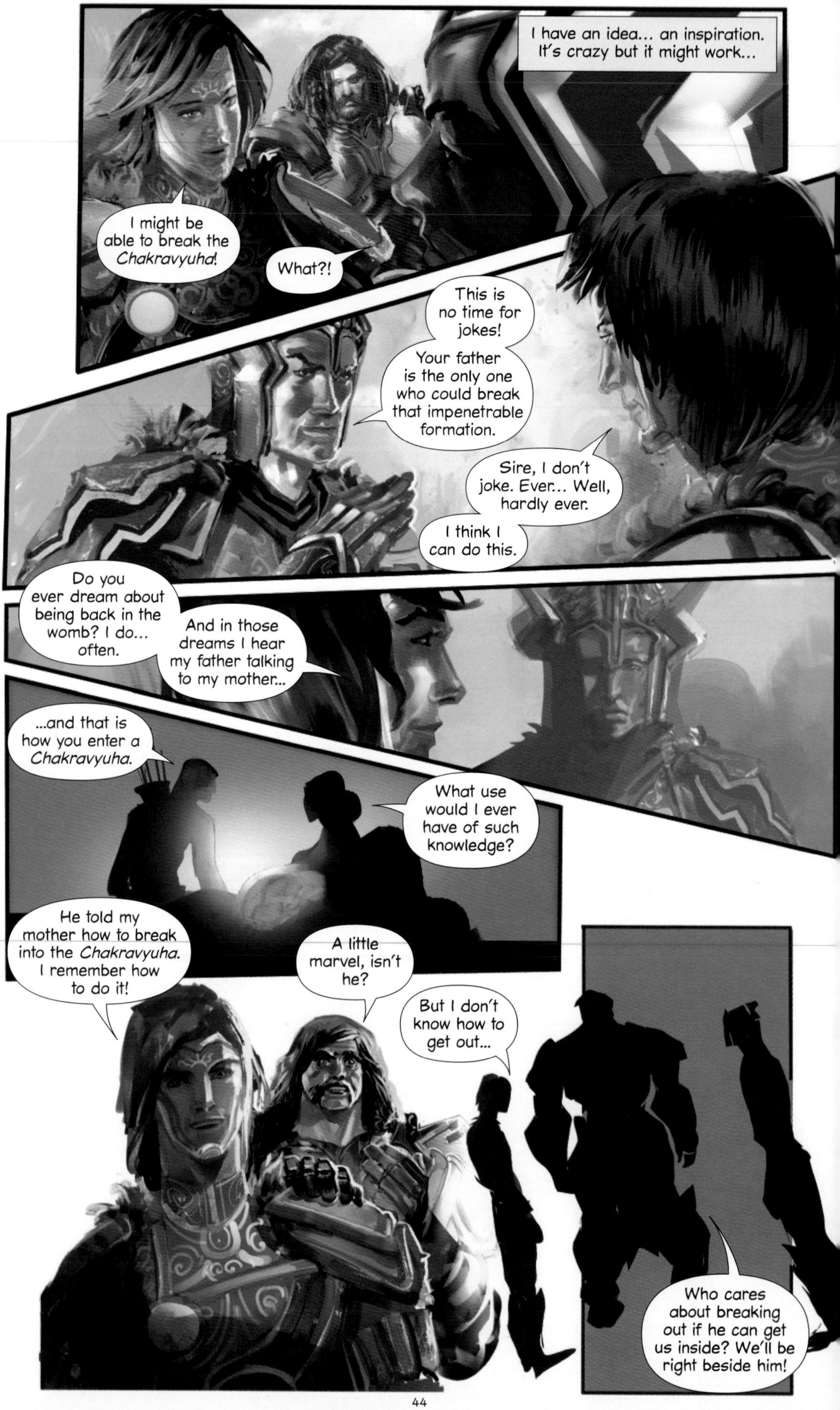
I have an idea... an inspiration. It's crazy but it might work...
I might be able to break the *Chakravyuha*!
What?!
This is no time for jokes!
Your father is the only one who could break that impenetrable formation.
Sire, I don't joke. Ever... Well, hardly ever.
I think I can do this.
Do you ever dream about being back in the womb? I do... often.
And in those dreams I hear my father talking to my mother...
...and that is how you enter a *Chakravyuha*.
What use would I ever have of such knowledge?
He told my mother how to break into the *Chakravyuha*. I remember how to do it!
A little marvel, isn't he?
But I don't know how to get out...
Who cares about breaking out if he can get us inside? We'll be right beside him!

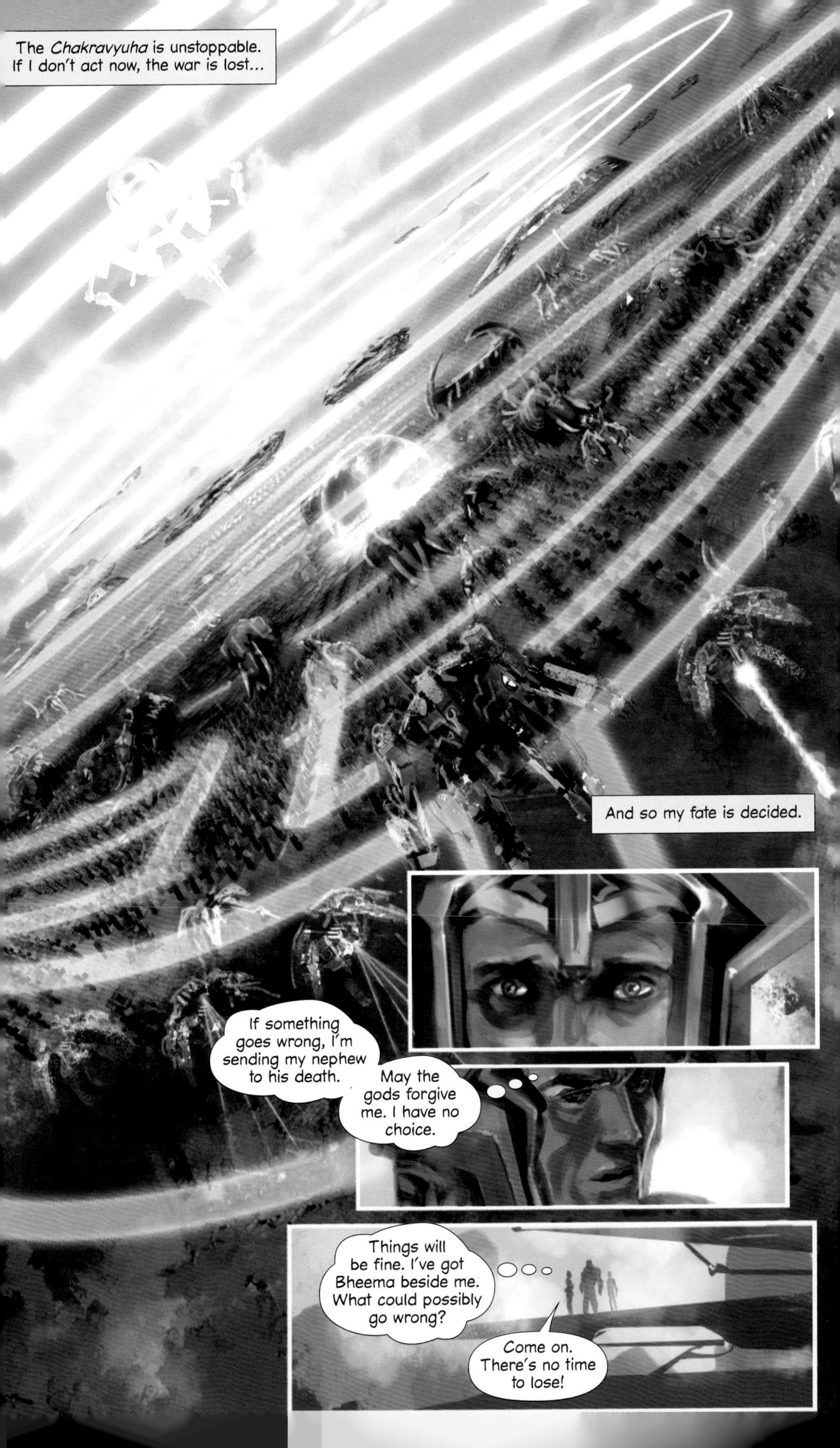
The *Chakravyuha* is unstoppable. If I don't act now, the war is lost...
And so my fate is decided.
If something goes wrong, I'm sending my nephew to his death.
May the gods forgive me. I have no choice.
Things will be fine. I've got Bheema beside me. What could possibly go wrong?
Come on. There's no time to lose!

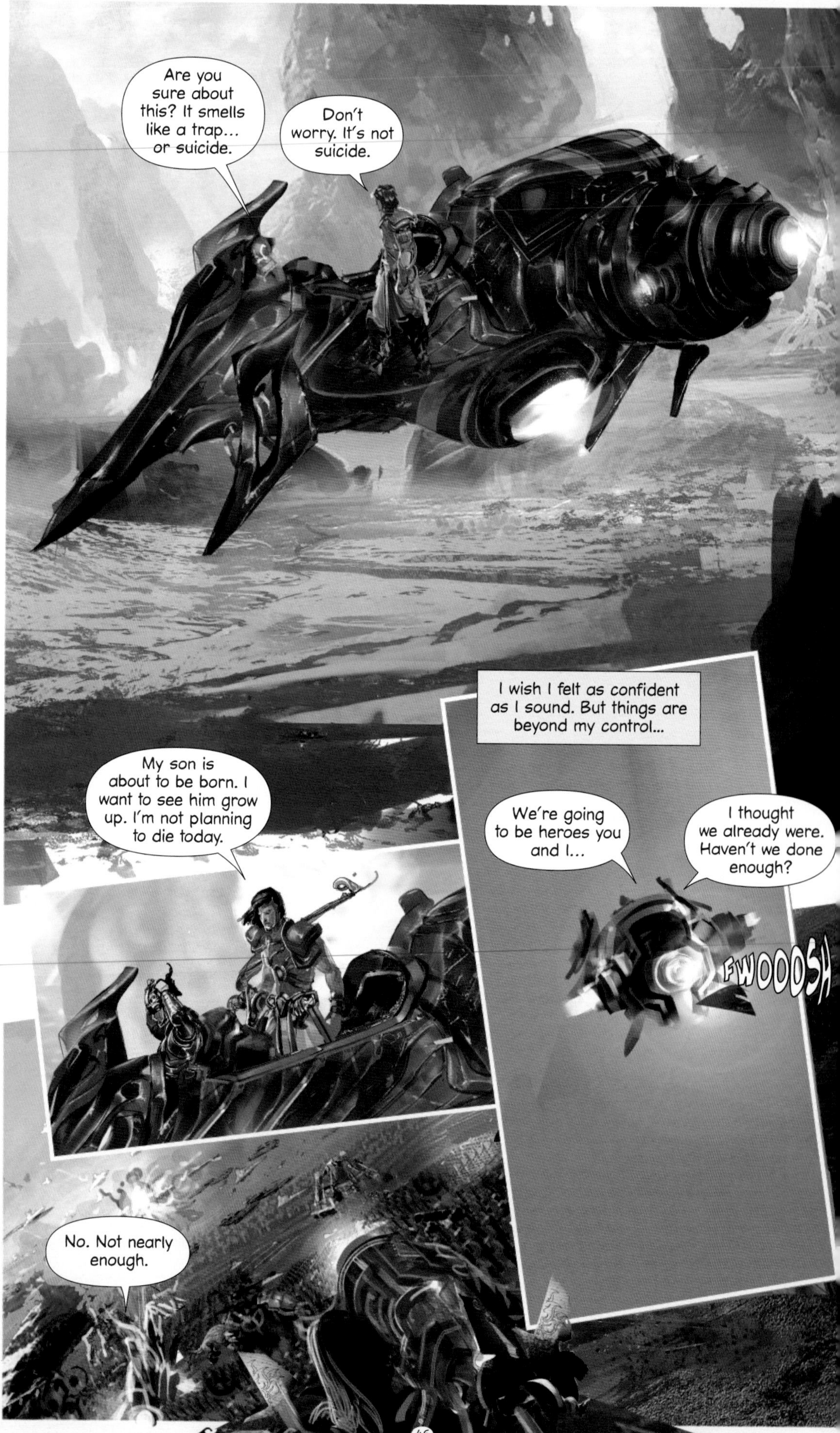

Are you sure about this? It smells like a trap... or suicide.
Don't worry. It's not suicide.
I wish I felt as confident as I sound. But things are beyond my control...
My son is about to be born. I want to see him grow up. I'm not planning to die today.
We're going to be heroes you and I...
I thought we already were. Haven't we done enough?
FWOOOSH
No. Not nearly enough.

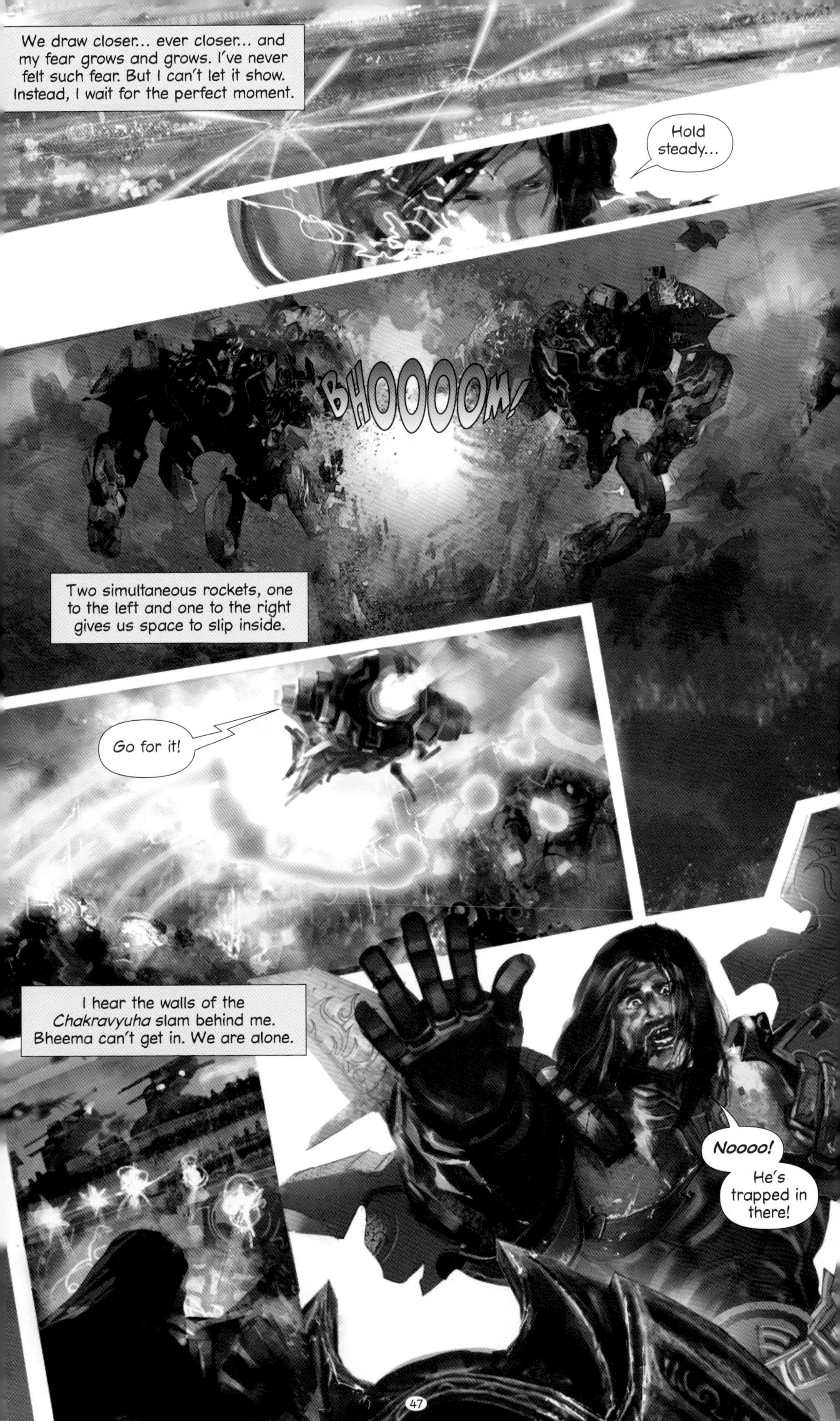

We draw closer... ever closer... and my fear grows and grows. I've never felt such fear. But I can't let it show. Instead, I wait for the perfect moment.
Hold steady...
BHOOOOM!
Two simultaneous rockets, one to the left and one to the right gives us space to slip inside.
Go for it!
I hear the walls of the *Chakravyuha* slam behind me. Bheema can't get in. We are alone.
Noooo!
He's trapped in there!

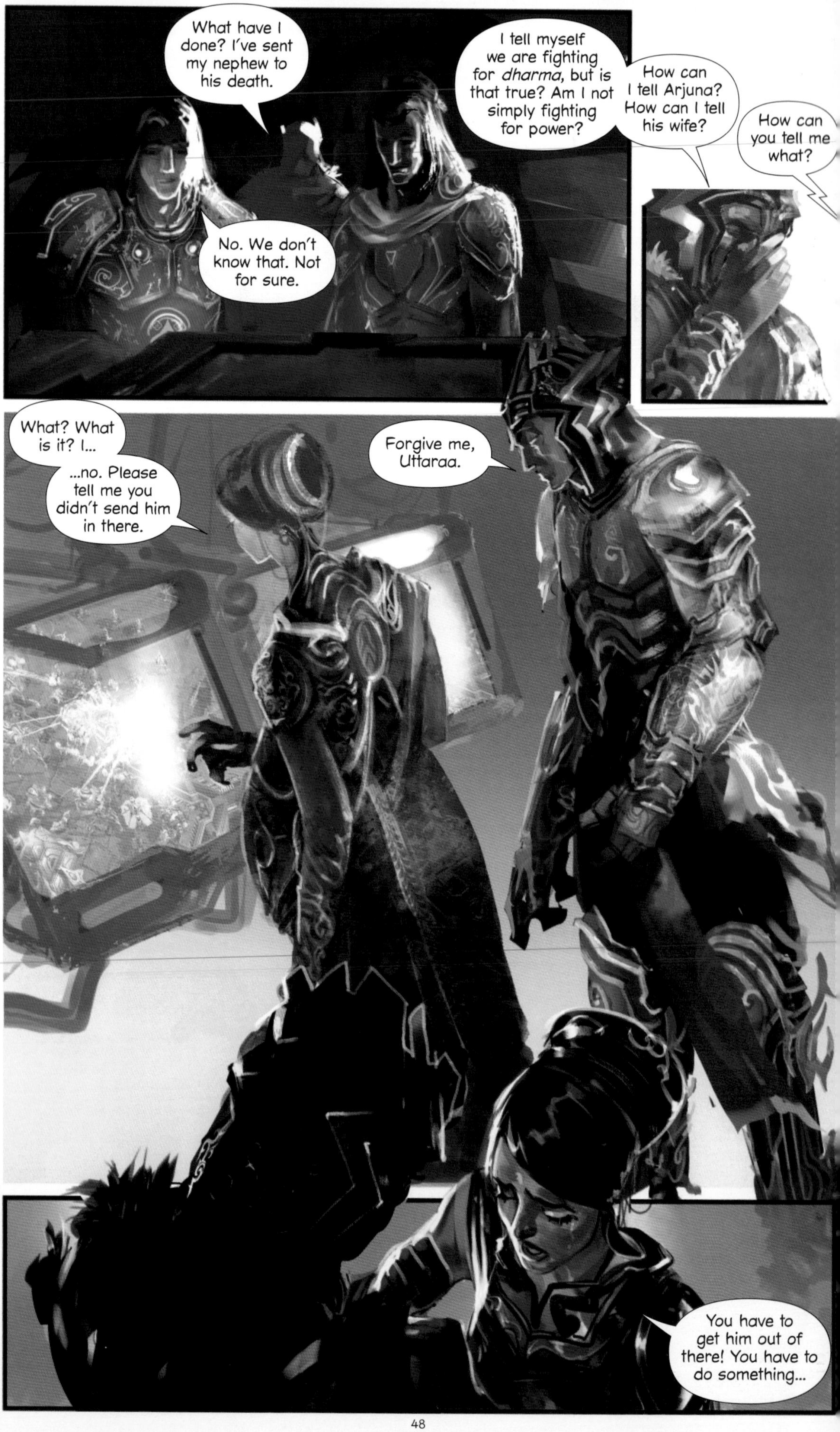
What have I done? I've sent my nephew to his death.
No. We don't know that. Not for sure.
I tell myself we are fighting for *dharma*, but is that true? Am I not simply fighting for power?
How can I tell Arjuna? How can I tell his wife?
How can you tell me what?
What? What is it? I...
...no. Please tell me you didn't send him in there.
Forgive me, Uttaraa.
You have to get him out of there! You have to do something...

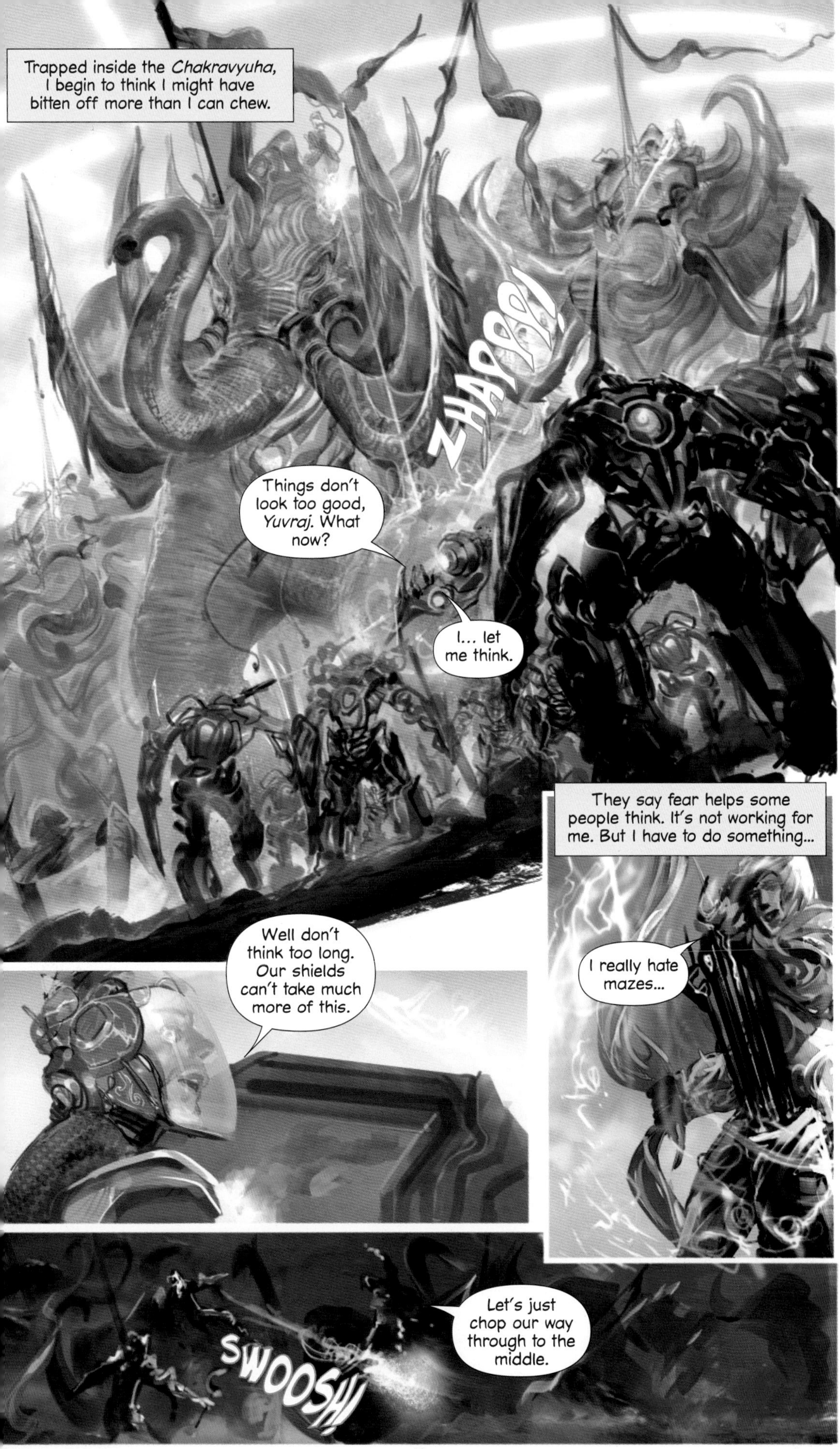
Trapped inside the *Chakravyuha*, I begin to think I might have bitten off more than I can chew.
ZHAPP!!
Things don't look too good, *Yuvraj*. What now?
I... let me think.
They say fear helps some people think. It's not working for me. But I have to do something...
Well don't think too long. Our shields can't take much more of this.
I really hate mazes...
Let's just chop our way through to the middle.
SWOOSH!

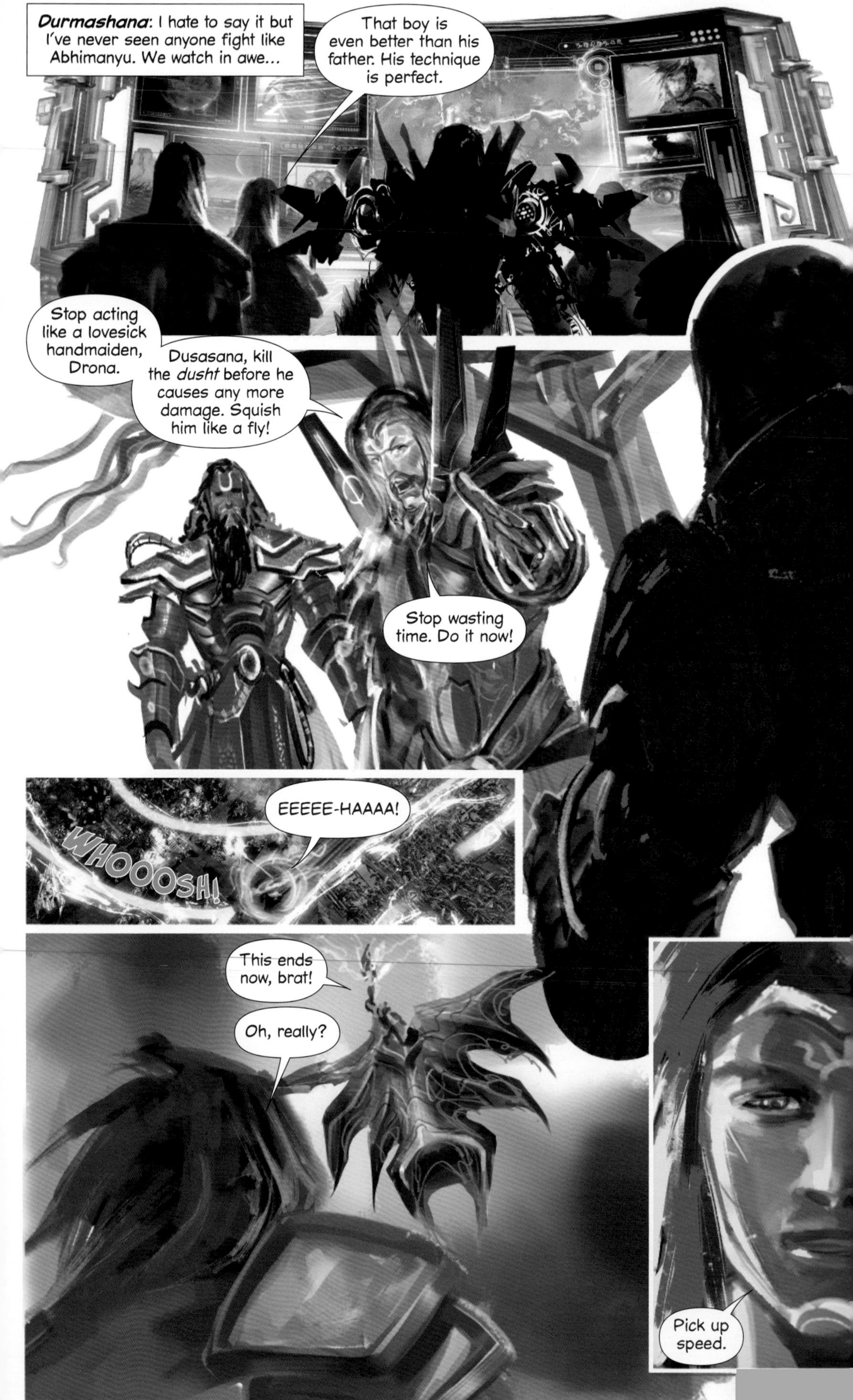
Durmashana: I hate to say it but I've never seen anyone fight like Abhimanyu. We watch in awe...
That boy is even better than his father. His technique is perfect.
Stop acting like a lovesick handmaiden, Drona.
Dusasana, kill the dusht before he causes any more damage. Squish him like a fly!
Stop wasting time. Do it now!
EEEEE-HAAAA!
WHOOOOSH!
This ends now, brat!
Oh, really?
Pick up speed.

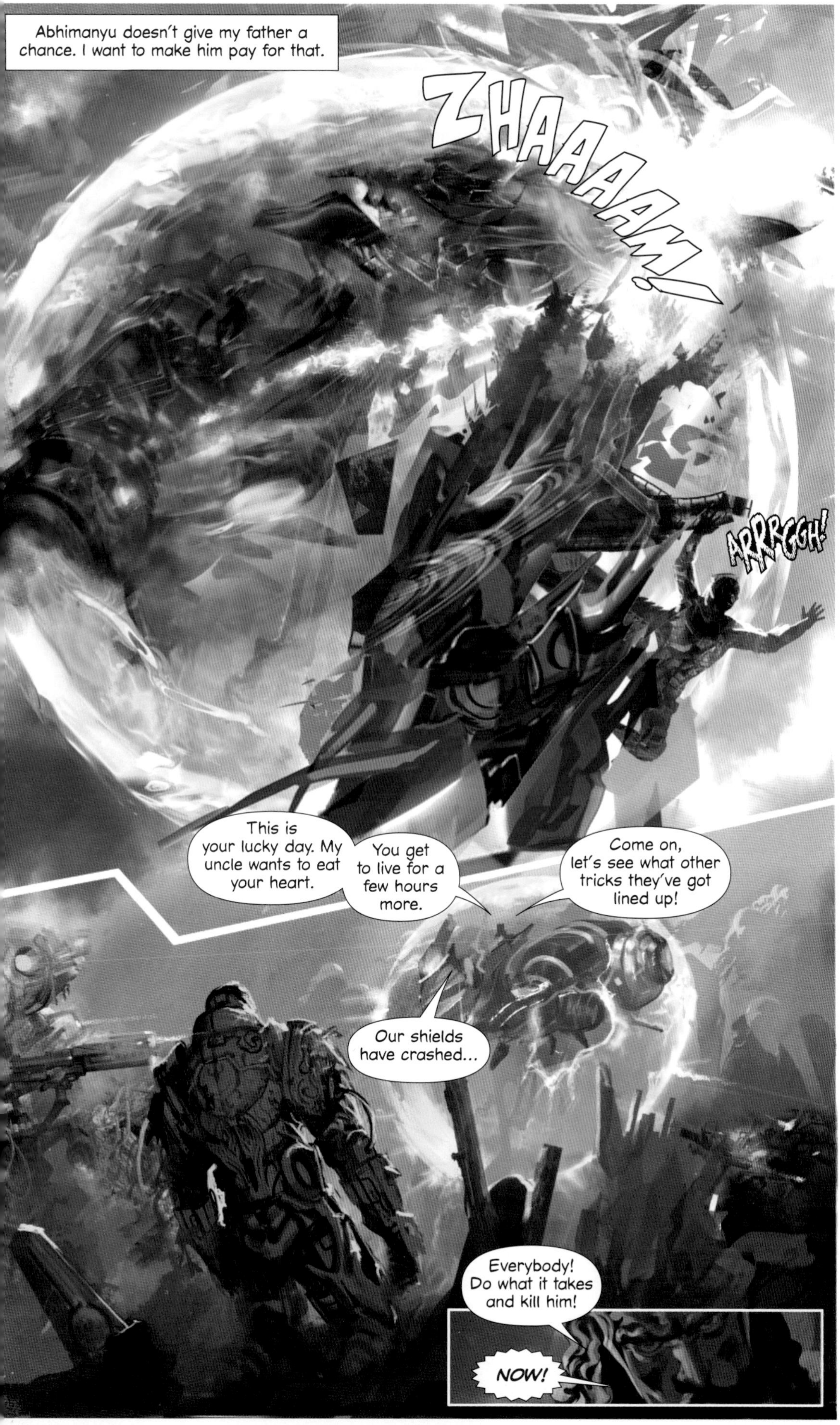

Abhimanyu doesn't give my father a chance. I want to make him pay for that.
ZHAAAAM!
ARRRGGH!
This is your lucky day. My uncle wants to eat your heart.
You get to live for a few hours more.
Come on, let's see what other tricks they've got lined up!
Our shields have crashed...
Everybody! Do what it takes and kill him!
NOW!

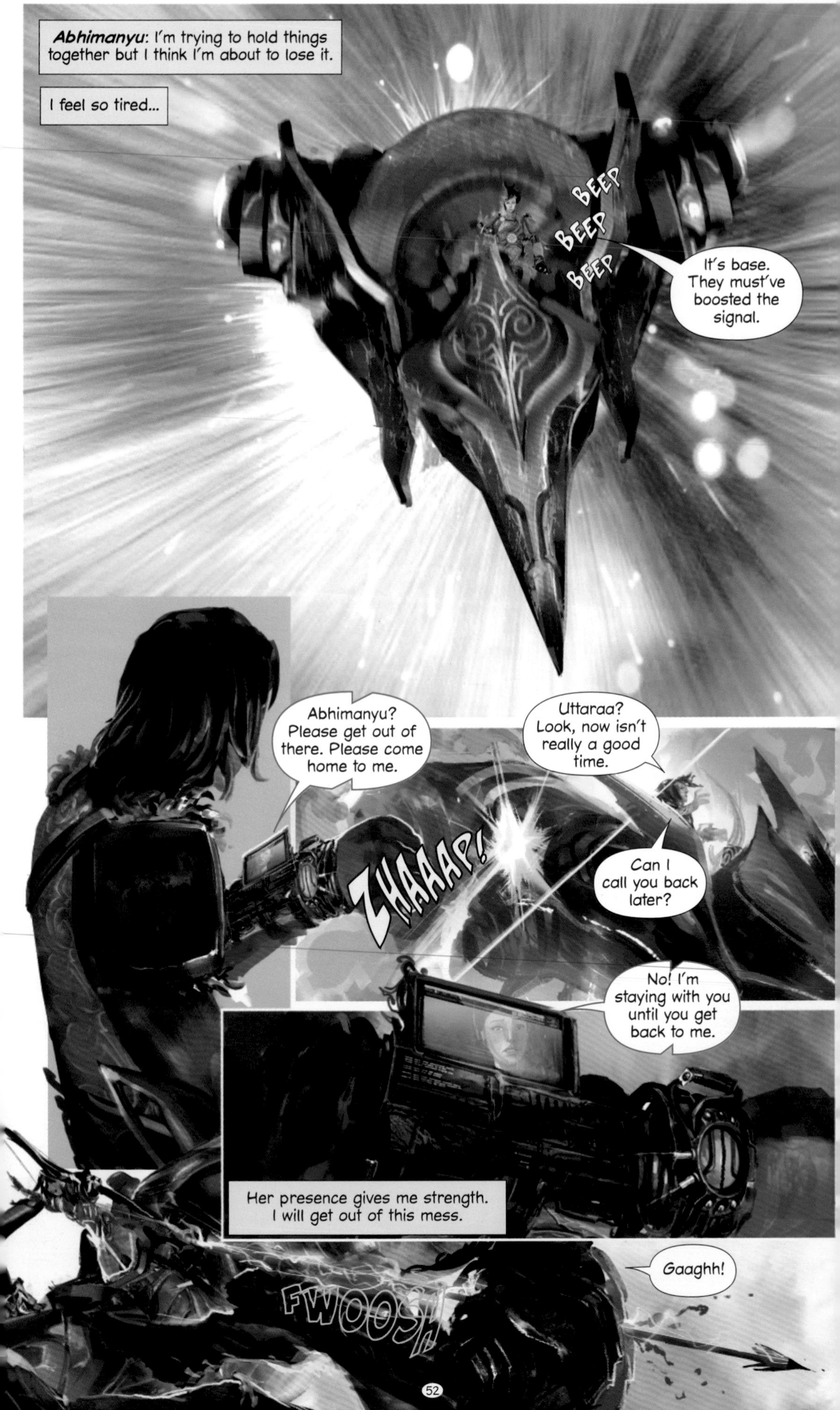
Abhimanyu: I'm trying to hold things together but I think I'm about to lose it.
I feel so tired...
BEEP BEEP BEEP
It's base. They must've boosted the signal.
Abhimanyu? Please get out of there. Please come home to me.
Uttaraa? Look, now isn't really a good time.
ZHAAAP!
Can I call you back later?
No! I'm staying with you until you get back to me.
Her presence gives me strength. I will get out of this mess.
Gaaghh!
FWOOSH

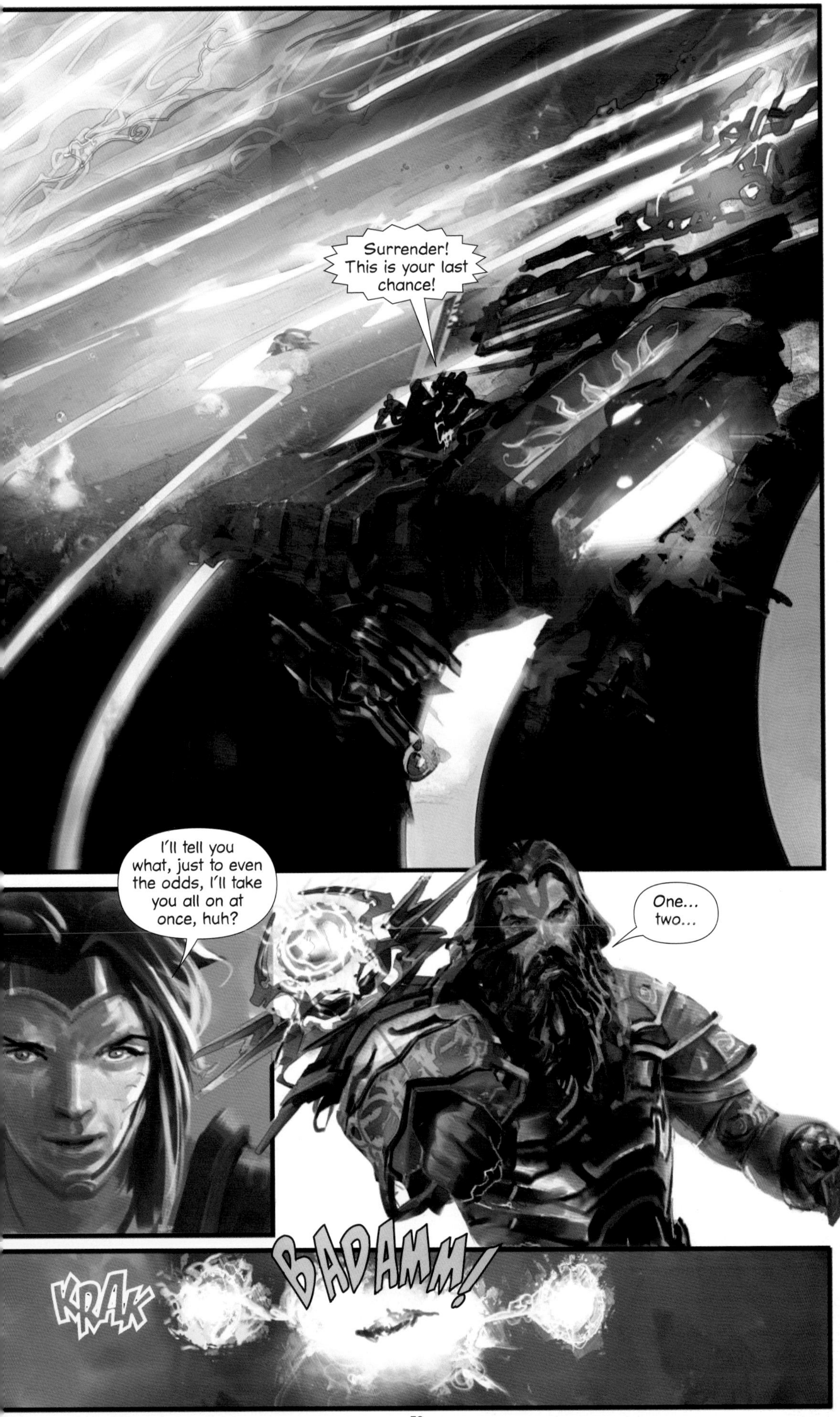

Surrender! This is your last chance!
I'll tell you what, just to even the odds, I'll take you all on at once, huh?
One... two...
KRAK
BADAMM!

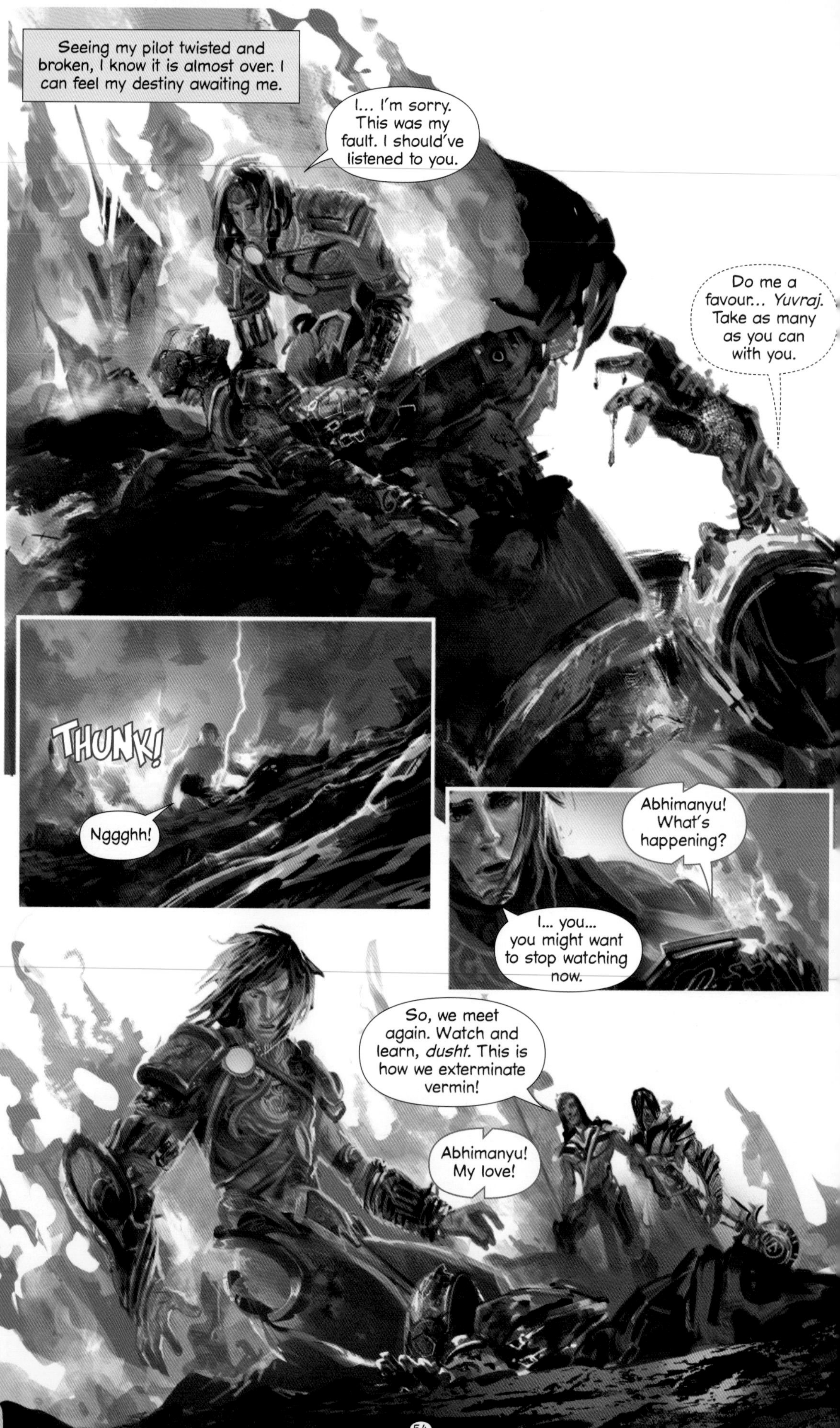
Seeing my pilot twisted and broken, I know it is almost over. I can feel my destiny awaiting me.
I... I'm sorry. This was my fault. I should've listened to you.
Do me a favour... *Yuvraj.* Take as many as you can with you.
THUNK!
Nggghh!
Abhimanyu! What's happening?
I... you... you might want to stop watching now.
So, we meet again. Watch and learn, *dusht.* This is how we exterminate vermin!
Abhimanyu! My love!

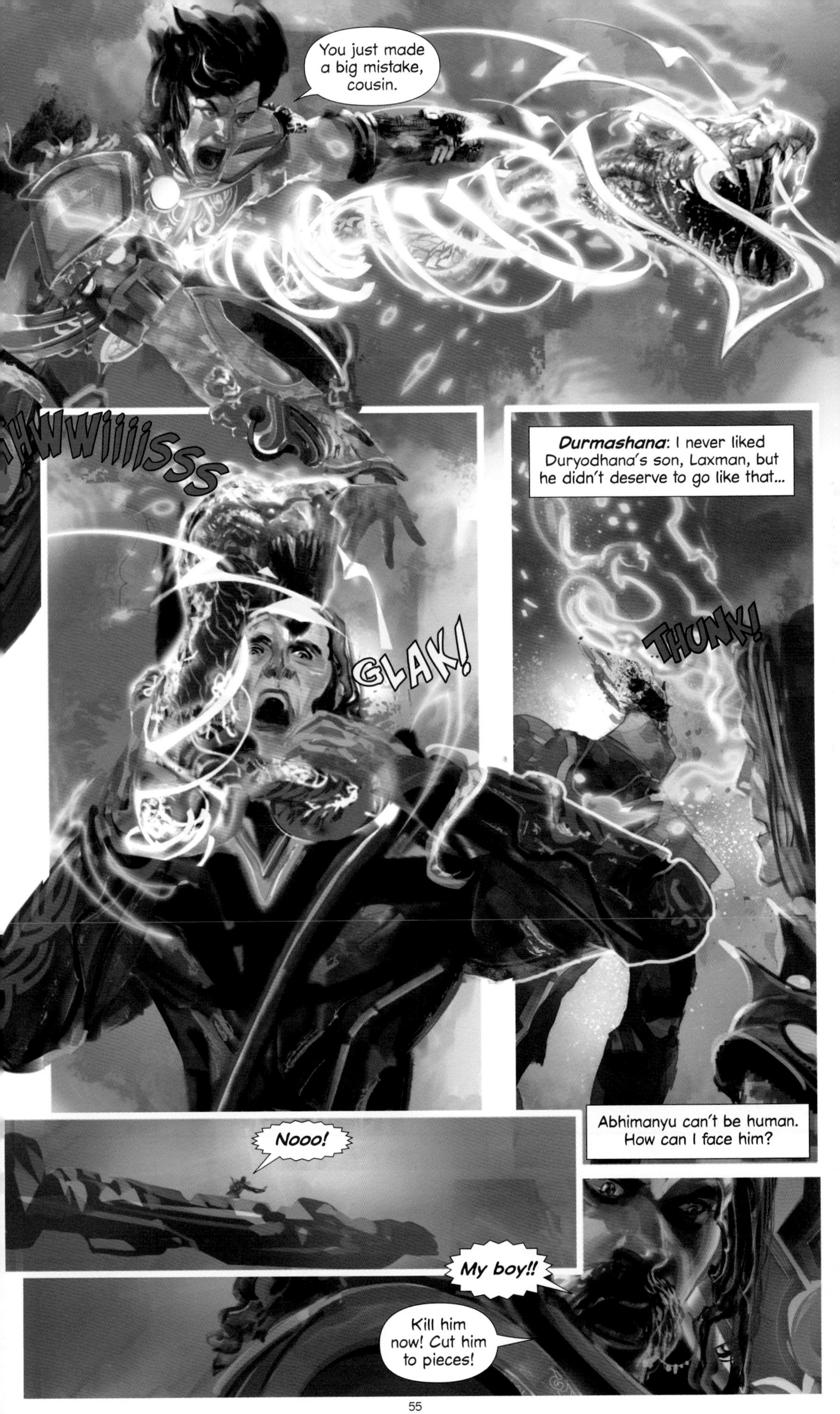

You just made a big mistake, cousin.
SHWWIIIIISSS
GLAK!
Durmashana: I never liked Duryodhana's son, Laxman, but he didn't deserve to go like that...
THUNK!
Abhimanyu can't be human. How can I face him?
Nooo!
My boy!!
Kill him now! Cut him to pieces!

He's killed Duryodhana's son. They...

Please, tell him to surrender! Order him! He won't listen to me.

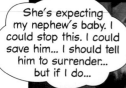

She's expecting my nephew's baby. I could stop this. I could save him... I should tell him to surrender... but if I do...

Can I do this? This is bigger than one man. The future of the Empire is at stake.

He... he's sixteen years old. He's got his whole life ahead of him.

Please...

Abhimanyu! Surrender now! Before it's too late.

No!

Surrender! Please!

I wish I could. But my destiny has to be fulfilled!

AAHH!

ZZZZAAAP!

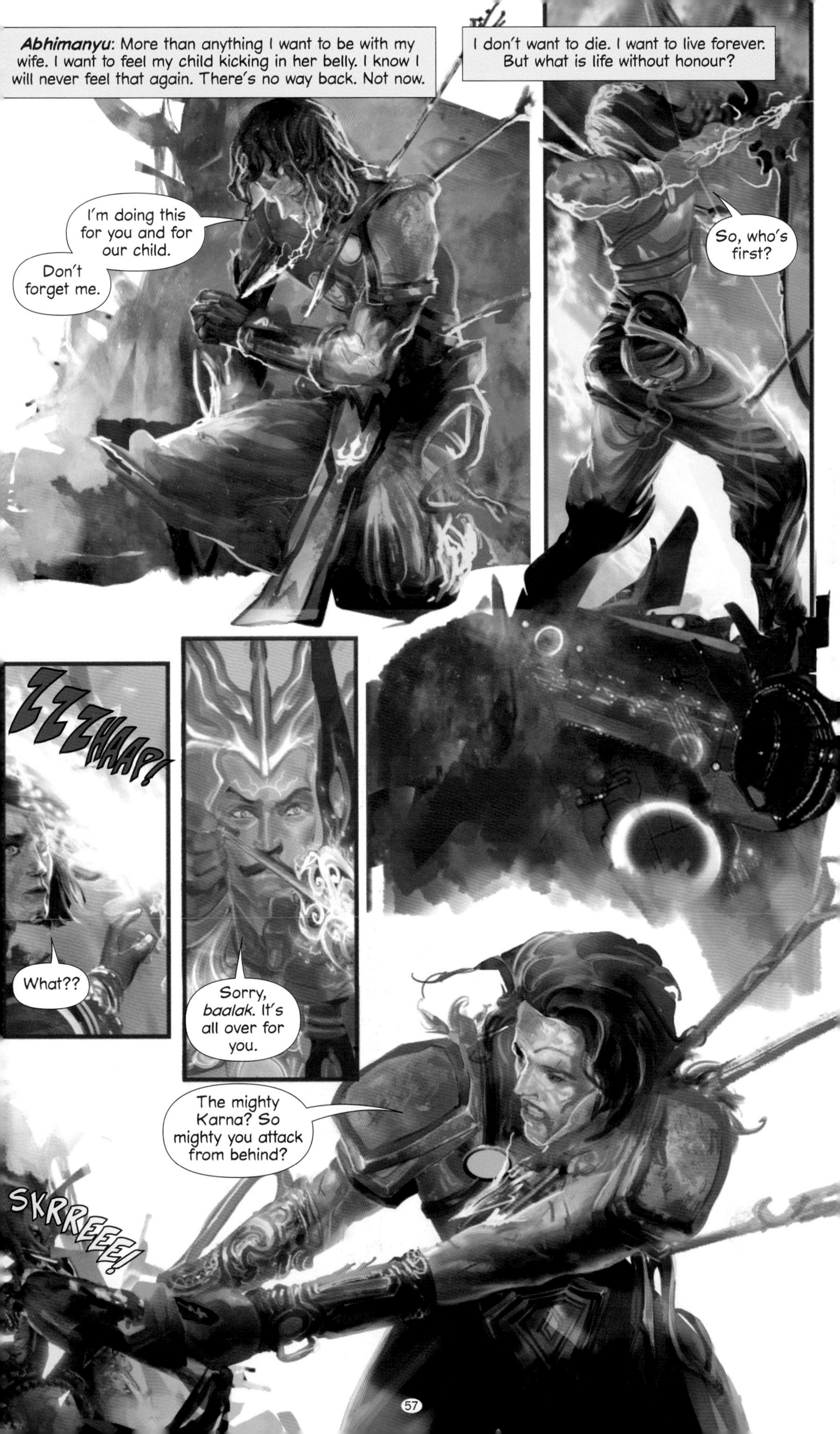
Abhimanyu: More than anything I want to be with my wife. I want to feel my child kicking in her belly. I know I will never feel that again. There's no way back. Not now.
I'm doing this for you and for our child.
Don't forget me.
I don't want to die. I want to live forever. But what is life without honour?
So, who's first?
ZZZHAAP!
What??
Sorry, baalak. It's all over for you.
The mighty Karna? So mighty you attack from behind?
SKRREEEE!

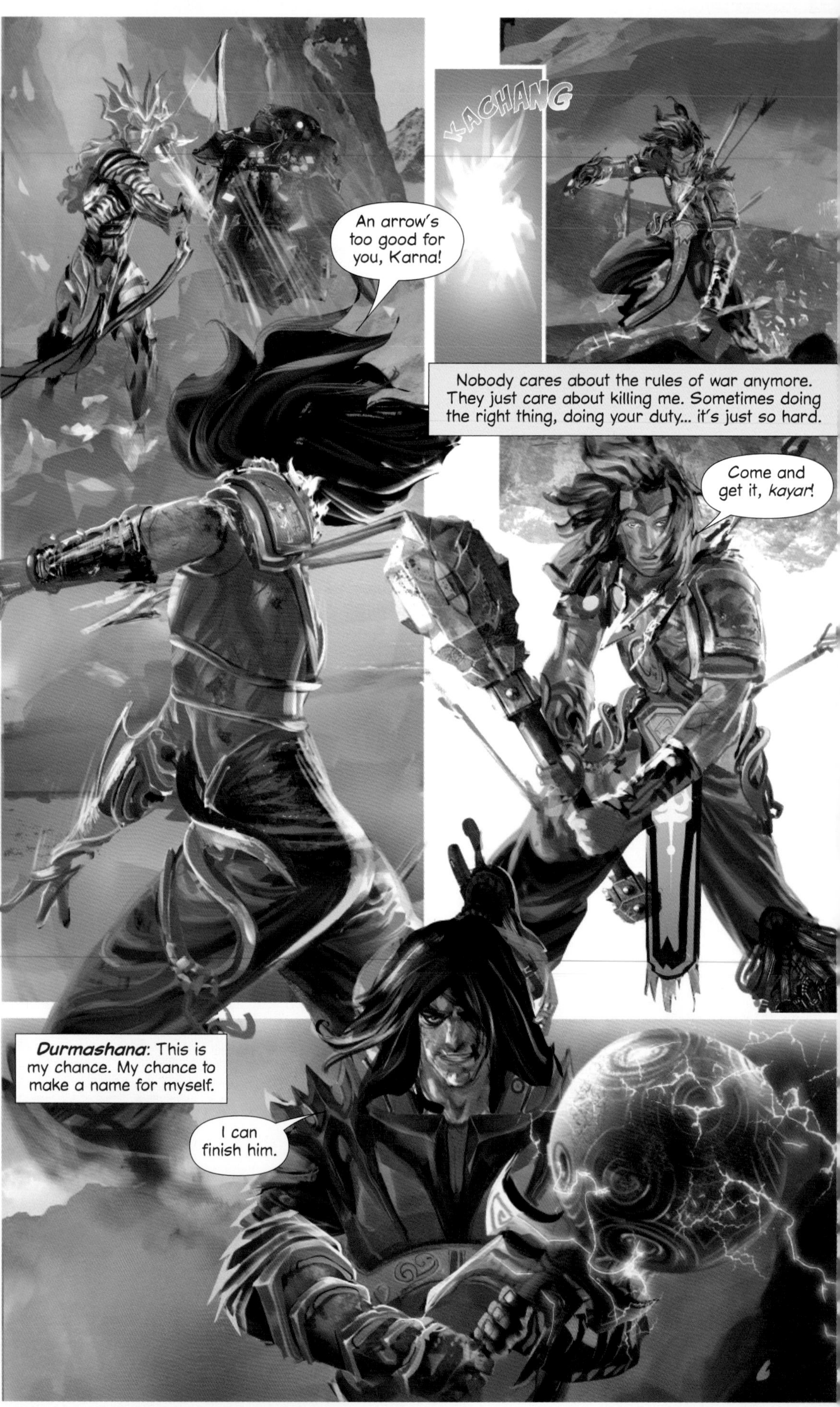
KACHANG
An arrow's too good for you, Karna!
Nobody cares about the rules of war anymore. They just care about killing me. Sometimes doing the right thing, doing your duty... it's just so hard.
Come and get it, *kayar*!
Durmashana: This is my chance. My chance to make a name for myself.
I can finish him.

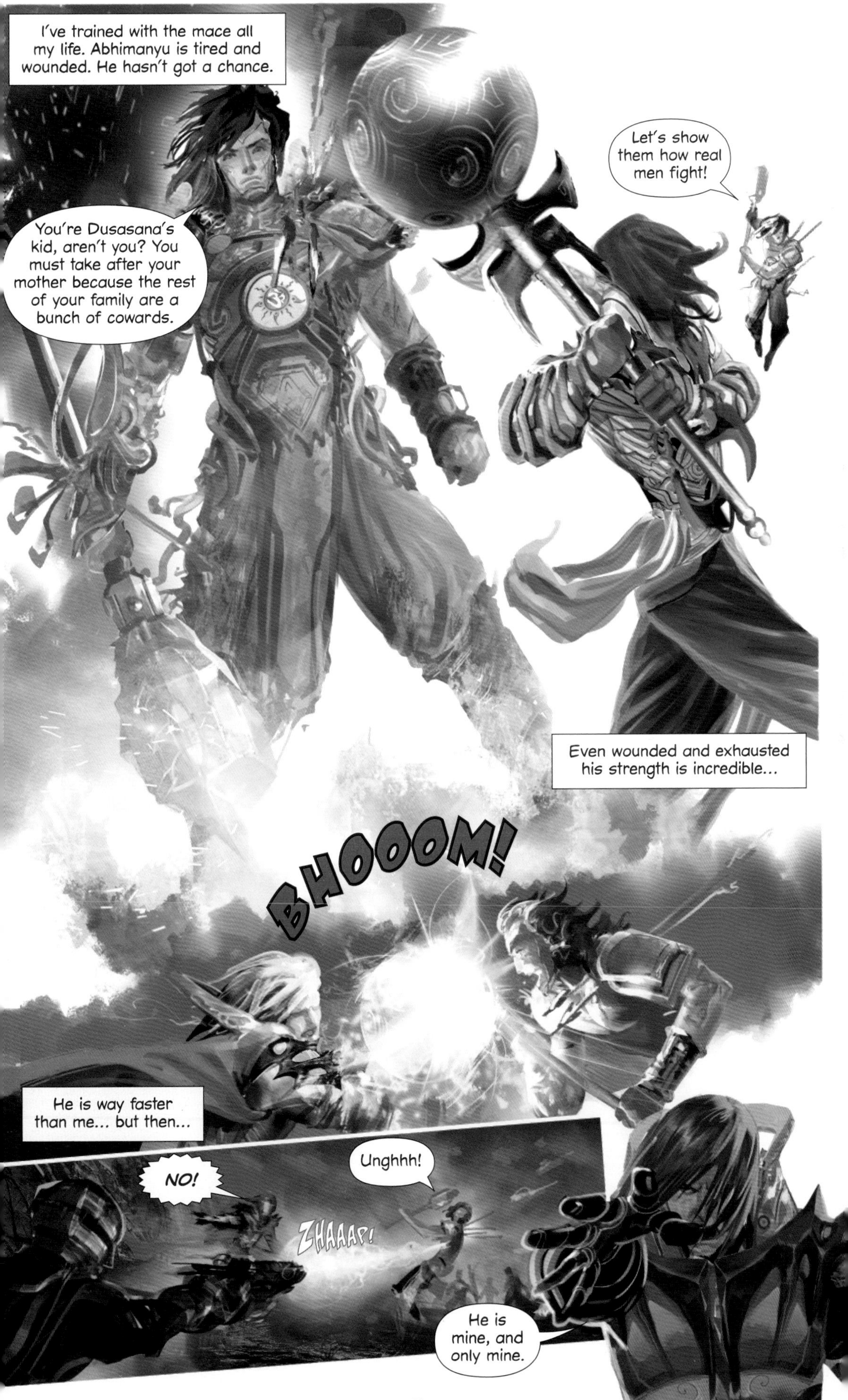
I've trained with the mace all my life. Abhimanyu is tired and wounded. He hasn't got a chance.
Let's show them how real men fight!
You're Dusasana's kid, aren't you? You must take after your mother because the rest of your family are a bunch of cowards.
Even wounded and exhausted his strength is incredible...
BHOOOM!
He is way faster than me... but then...
NO!
Unghhh!
ZHAAAP!
He is mine, and only mine.

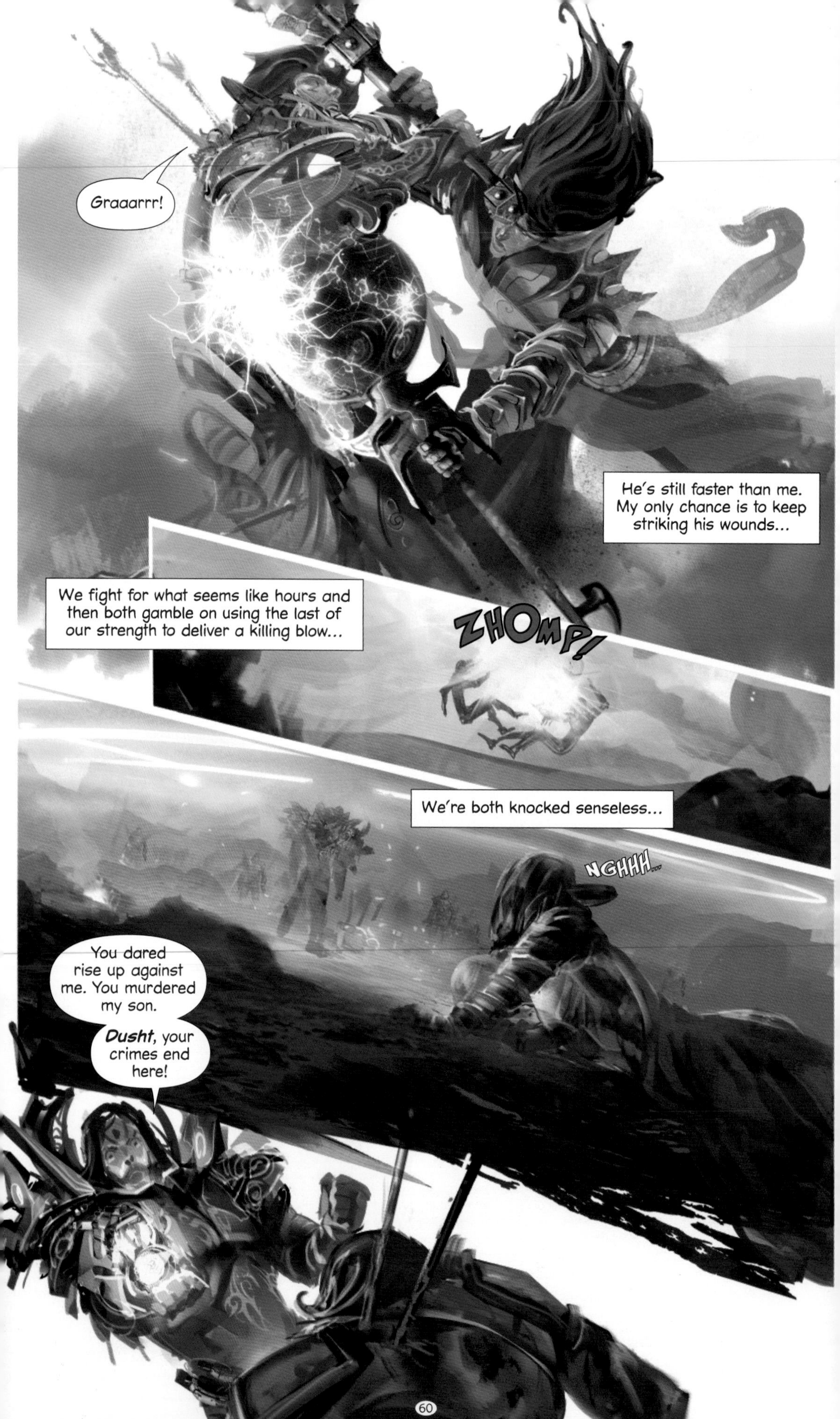
Graaarrr!
He's still faster than me. My only chance is to keep striking his wounds...
We fight for what seems like hours and then both gamble on using the last of our strength to deliver a killing blow...
ZHOMP!
We're both knocked senseless...
NGHHH...
You dared rise up against me. You murdered my son.
Dusht, your crimes end here!

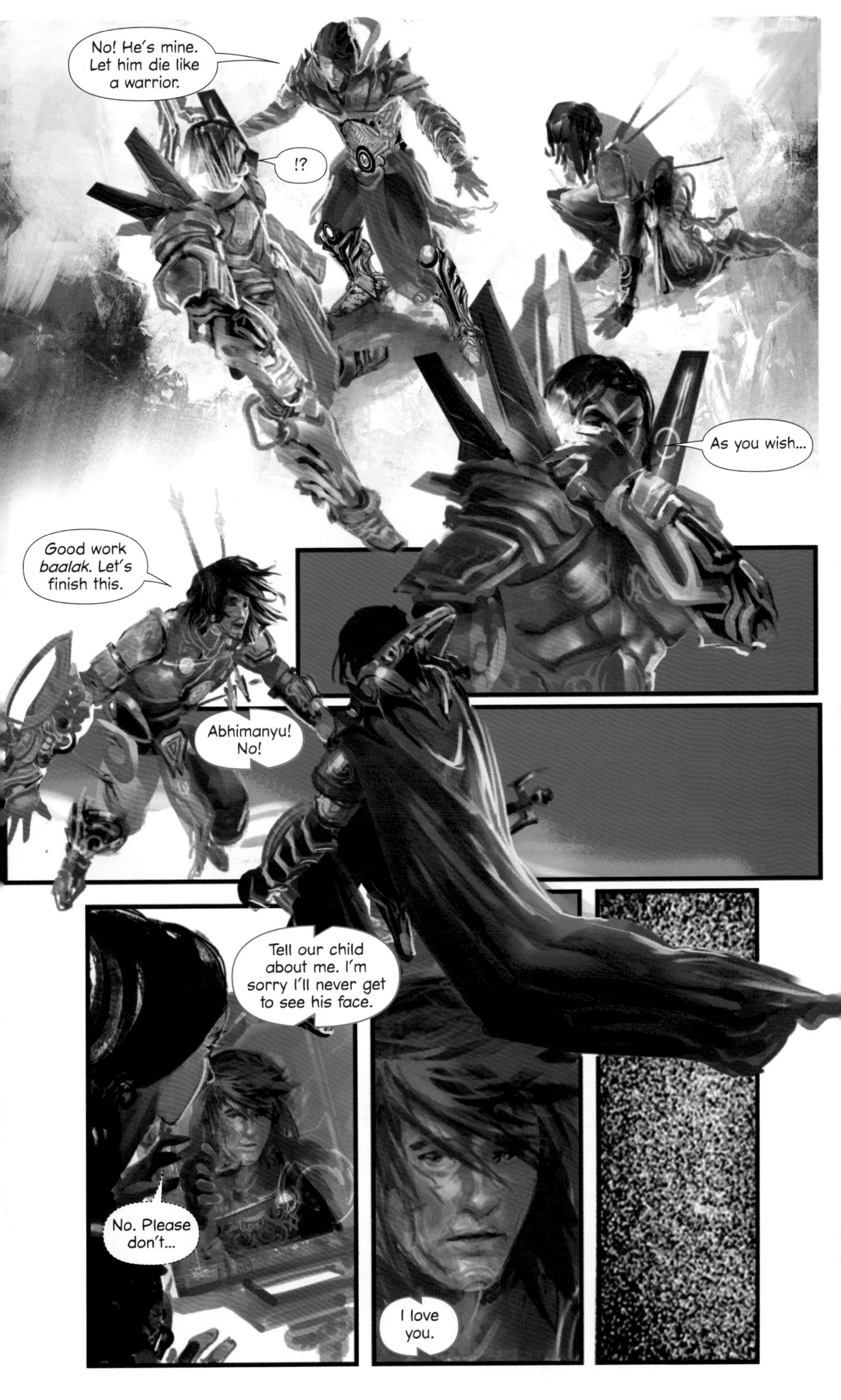

No! He's mine. Let him die like a warrior.
!?
As you wish...
Good work *baalak*. Let's finish this.
Abhimanyu! No!
Tell our child about me. I'm sorry I'll never get to see his face.
No. Please don't...
I love you.

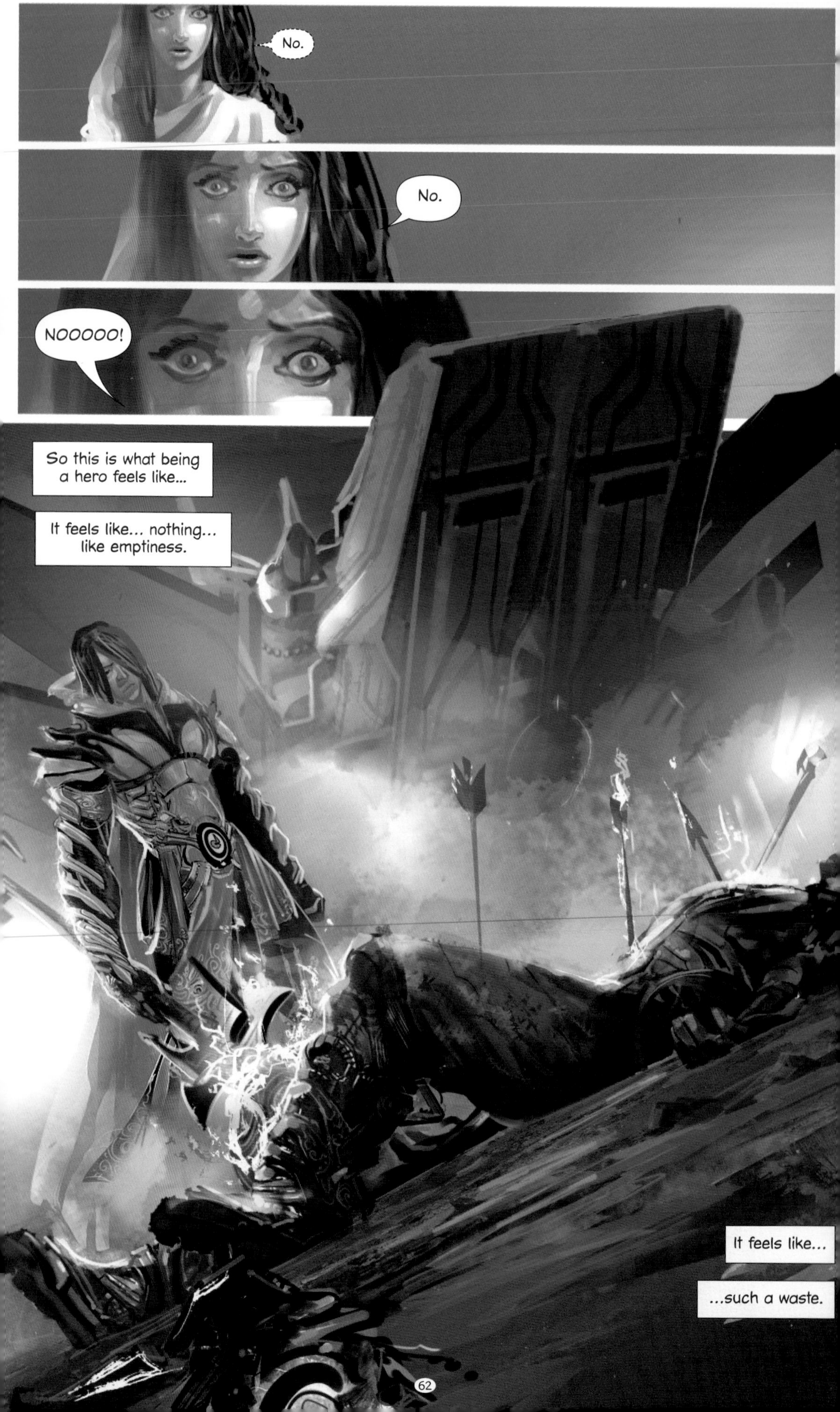
No.
No.
NOOOOO!
So this is what being a hero feels like...
It feels like... nothing... like emptiness.
It feels like...
...such a waste.

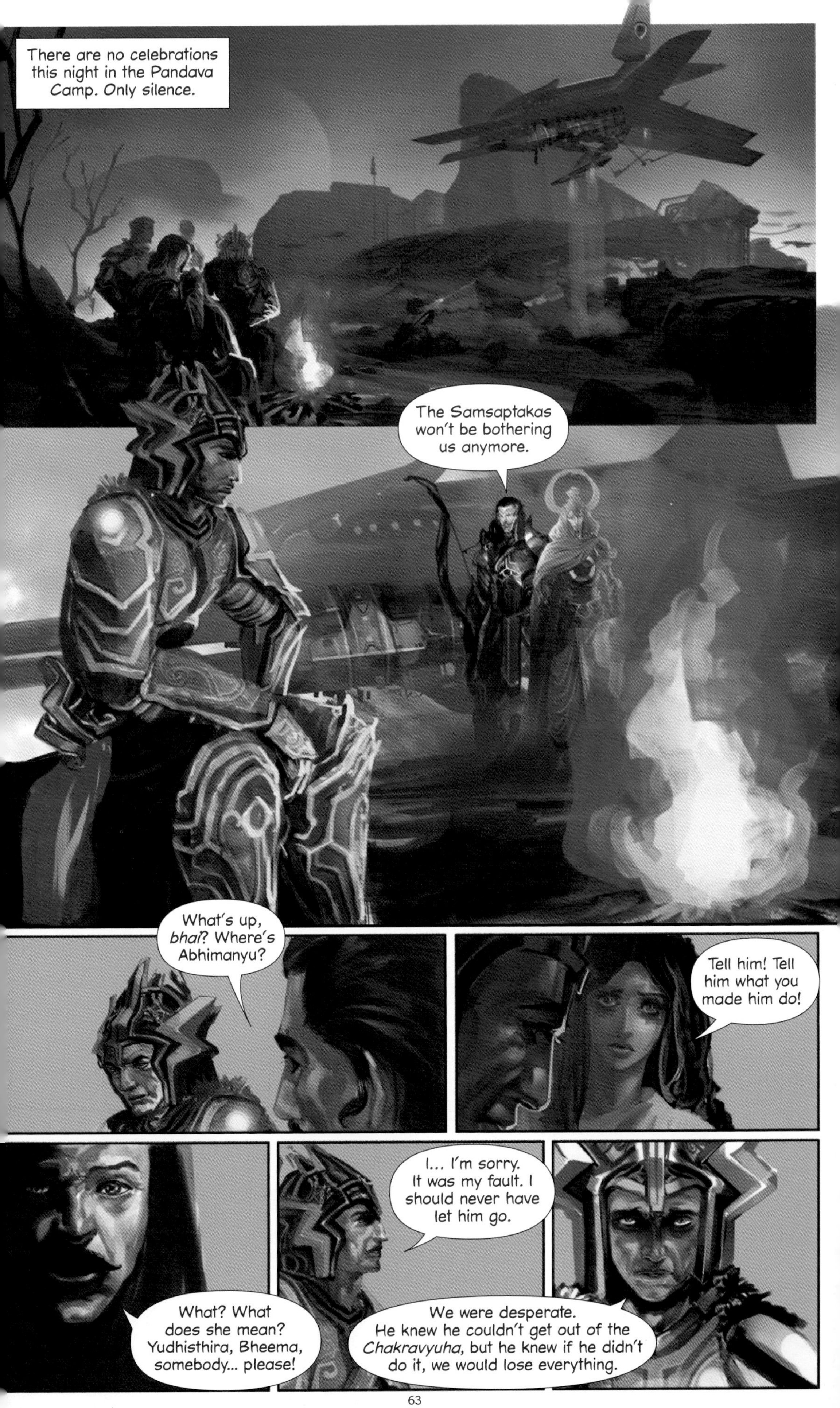
There are no celebrations this night in the Pandava Camp. Only silence.
The Samsaptakas won't be bothering us anymore.
What's up, *bhai*? Where's Abhimanyu?
Tell him! Tell him what you made him do!
I... I'm sorry. It was my fault. I should never have let him go.
What? What does she mean? Yudhisthira, Bheema, somebody... please!
We were desperate. He knew he couldn't get out of the *Chakravyuha*, but he knew if he didn't do it, we would lose everything.

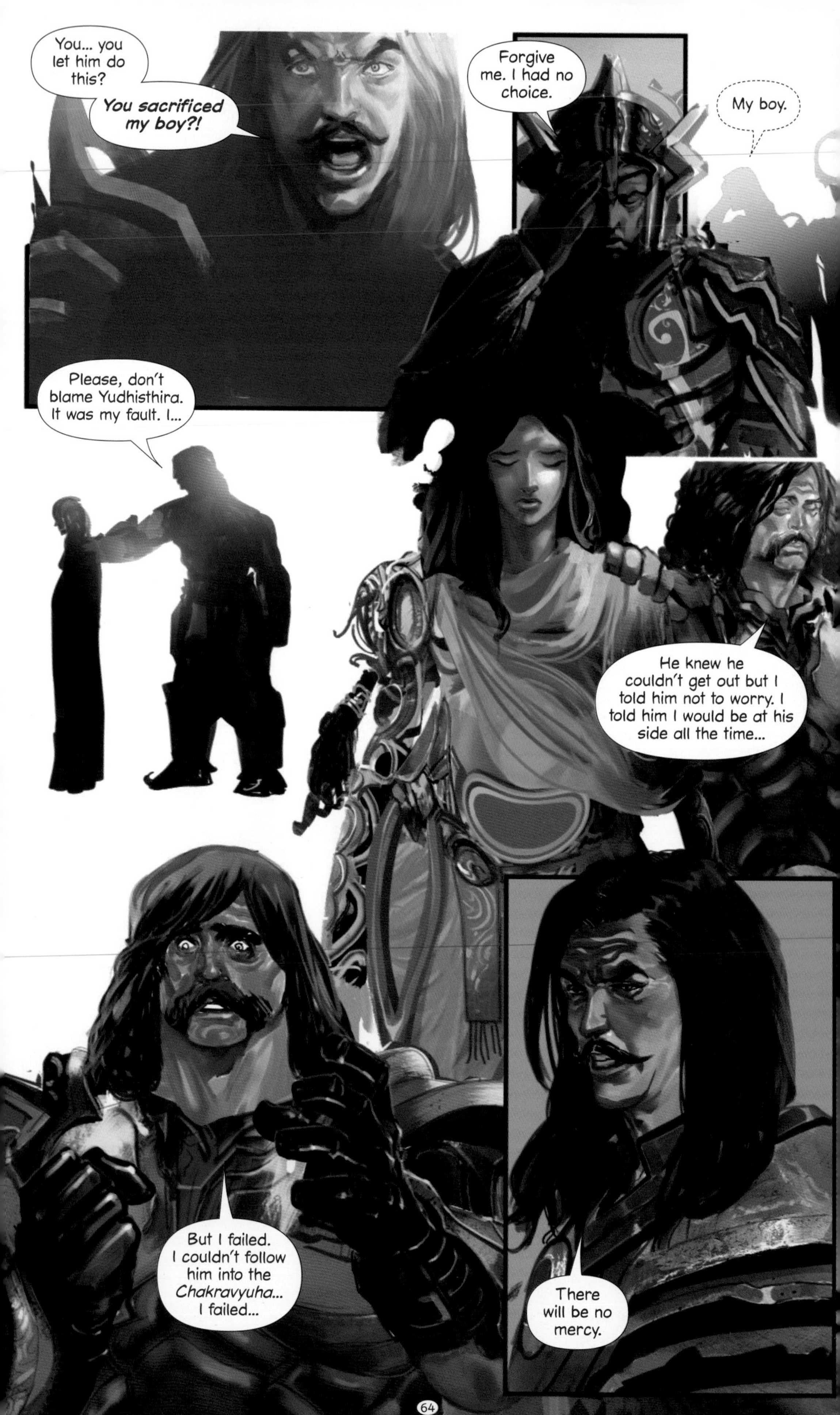
You... you let him do this?
You sacrificed my boy?!
Forgive me. I had no choice.
My boy.
Please, don't blame Yudhisthira. It was my fault. I...
He knew he couldn't get out but I told him not to worry. I told him I would be at his side all the time...
But I failed. I couldn't follow him into the *Chakravyuha*... I failed...
There will be no mercy.

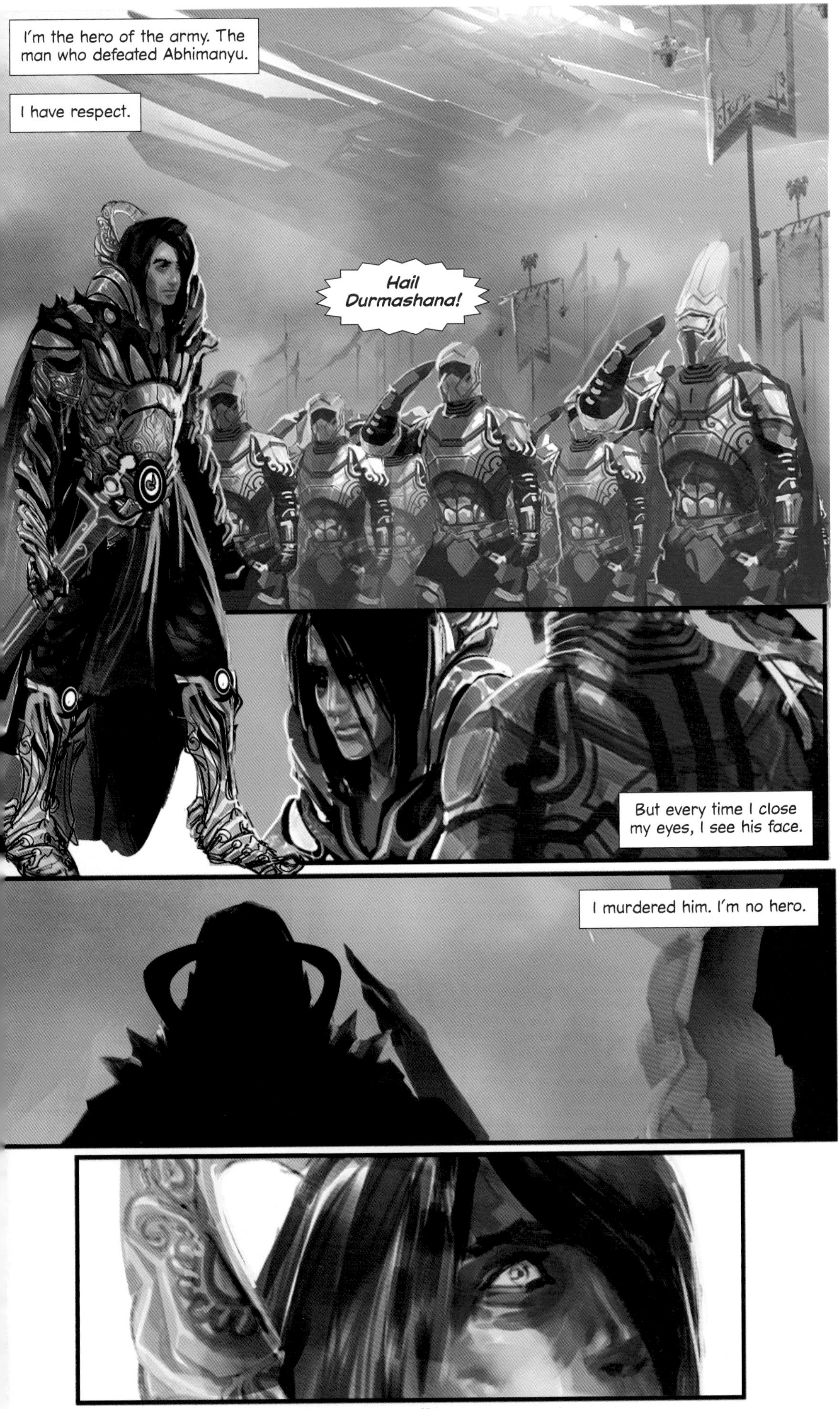
I'm the hero of the army. The man who defeated Abhimanyu.
I have respect.
Hail Durmashana!
But every time I close my eyes, I see his face.
I murdered him. I'm no hero.

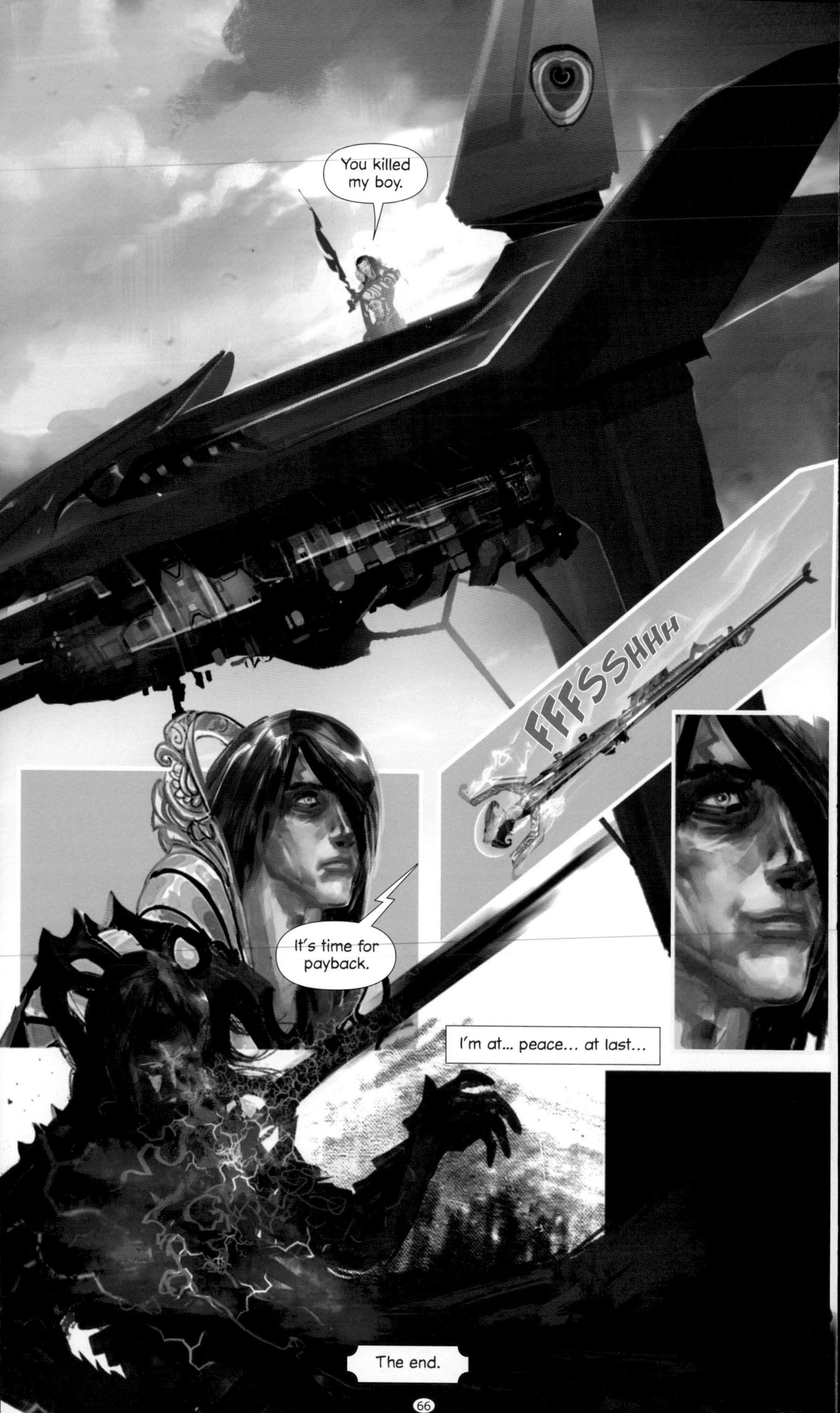
You killed my boy.
FFFSSHHH
It's time for payback.
I'm at... peace... at last...
The end.

THE KAURAVA EMPIRE

ABHIMANYU AND THE CONQUEST OF THE CHAKRAVYUHA

MAIN CHARACTERS

THE KAURAVA EMPIRE HAS A CAST OF THOUSANDS AND TO GIVE YOU A FULL CHARACTER BREAKDOWN ON ALL OUR STELLAR CAST WOULD REQUIRE YET ANOTHER VOLUME ALL OF ITS OWN, SO INSTEAD, LET'S TAKE A LOOK AT SOME OF THIS BOOK'S MAJOR STARS!

⚔ ABHIMANYU

Abhimanyu is the perfect hero. He's brave, he's good looking, and on the battlefield he is virtually unstoppable. Abhimanyu is every bit as gifted with a bow as his father Arjuna, the greatest archer in the Empire, and if that isn't enough to impress you, think on this, he's only sixteen years of age! He would risk everything for his family and has absolute faith in his own abilities. In fact, when called upon to face the mightiest warriors in the Kaurava army, he has little doubt in his ability to take them all on. The warriors on both side of the great war are all in awe of Abhimanyu and rightly so.

⚔ DURMASHANA

Durmashana is the same age as his Pandava cousin, Abhimanyu, but he's not in the same league as a fighter. The son of Prince Dusasana, Durmashana is often mocked by his cousins and fellow Kauravas as a wannabe hero. He is envious of Abhimanyu's reputation and success on the battlefield and is determined to make a name for himself by being the one to beat him in combat. He is pretty handy with a power mace, and he believes firmly in the Kaurava cause. He longs for fame and glory, and is not afraid to punch above his weight when it comes to taking on an opponent.

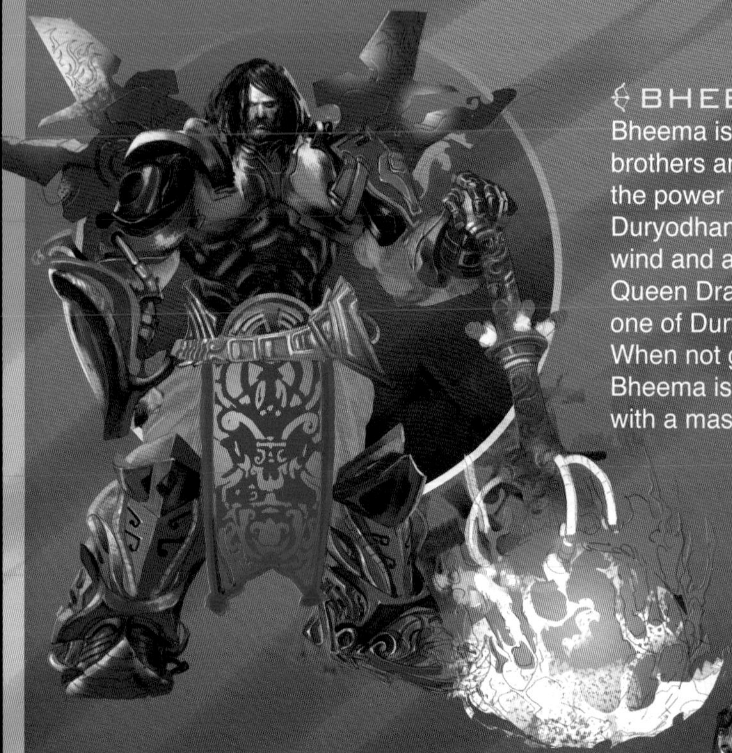

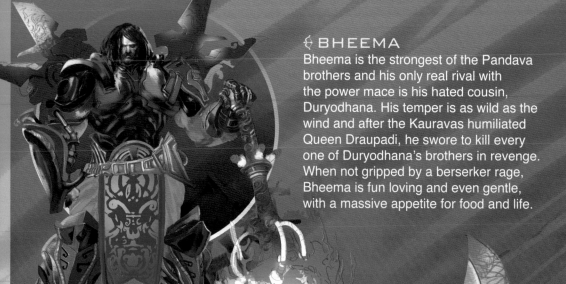

BHEEMA
Bheema is the strongest of the Pandava brothers and his only real rival with the power mace is his hated cousin, Duryodhana. His temper is as wild as the wind and after the Kauravas humiliated Queen Draupadi, he swore to kill every one of Duryodhana's brothers in revenge. When not gripped by a berserker rage, Bheema is fun loving and even gentle, with a massive appetite for food and life.

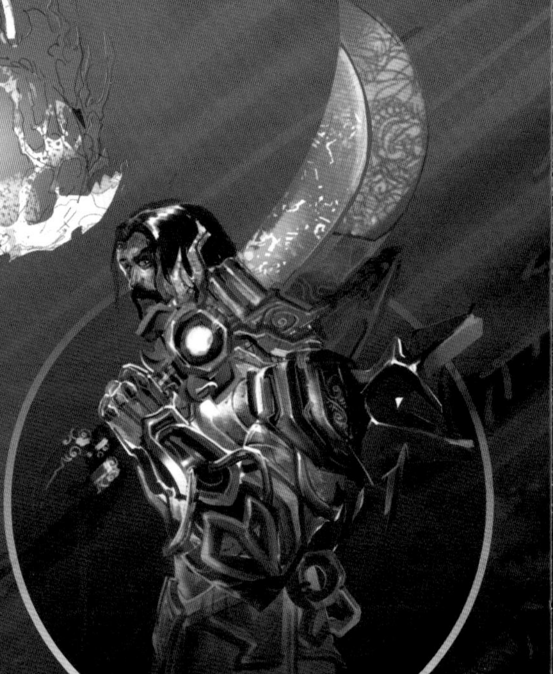

DURYODHANA
Crown Prince Duryodhana believed he would inherit the throne of the Kaurava Empire, until the arrival in Hastinapura of his cousins, the five Pandava brothers. After being informed that he would have to share power with his cousin Yudhisthira, Duryodhana began plotting their downfall. In most ways, he is a fair and noble prince, but his hatred of the Pandavas, and his cousin Bheema in particular, makes him rash, unreasonable and reckless. He would risk anything in order to preserve his power and vanquish his enemies.

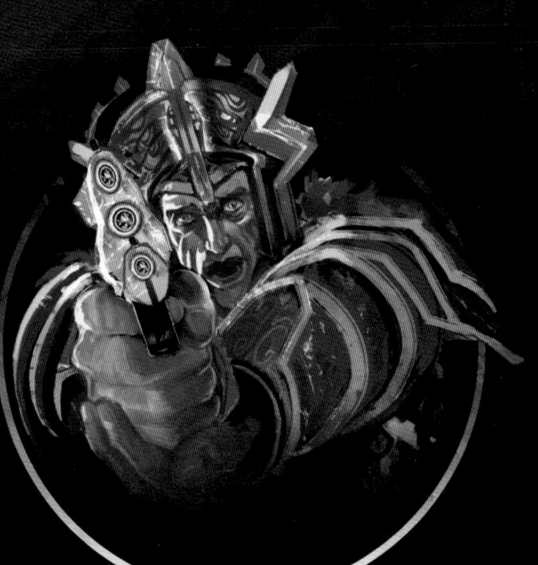

YUDHISTHIRA
The eldest of the five Pandava brothers, Yudhisthira, is the figurehead behind which the rebel forces have rallied to take on the might of the Kaurava Empire. Some people believe he is weak and indecisive, but Yudhisthira truly hates the carnage of war and in many ways he would be happier living a life of peace and tranquillity rather than ruling the known universe. Duryodhana's plots against his life and the lives of his family have shown him that the universe is not big enough for both the Kauravas and the Pandavas.

BHISHMA

Bhishma is the patriarch of both the Kaurava and Pandava clans. Nobody knows how old he is, but everybody fears him in battle. He has sworn to defend the Empire and so he fights for Duryodhana, as Commander-in-Chief of the Kaurava Forces. However, even in the middle of this all out war, he still loves the Pandavas and does his best to avoid facing them personally in battle.

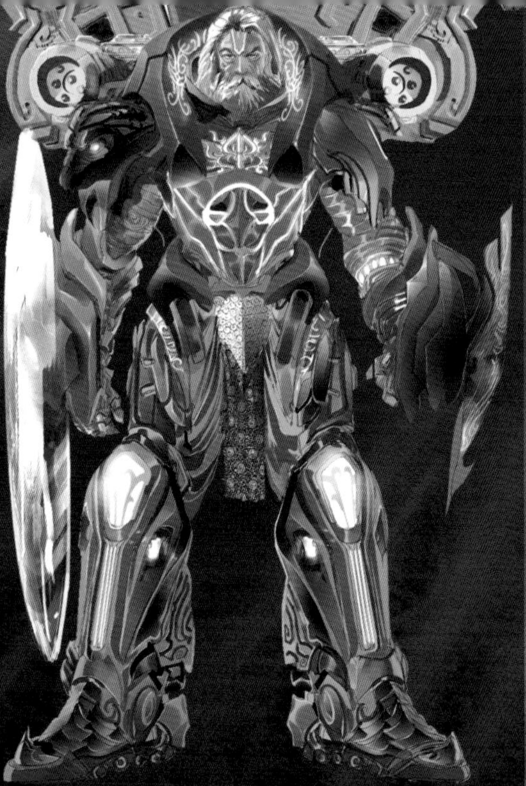

UTTARAA

Uttaraa is the teen-age wife of Abhimanyu. She herself is a princess and refuses to wait at home while her husband fights alongside his family. Heavily pregnant with Abhimanyu's child, Uttaraa has every confidence in her young husband's abilities on the battlefield. She is brave, loyal and has an infinite zest for life. She enjoys teasing her husband and is never afraid to speak her mind.

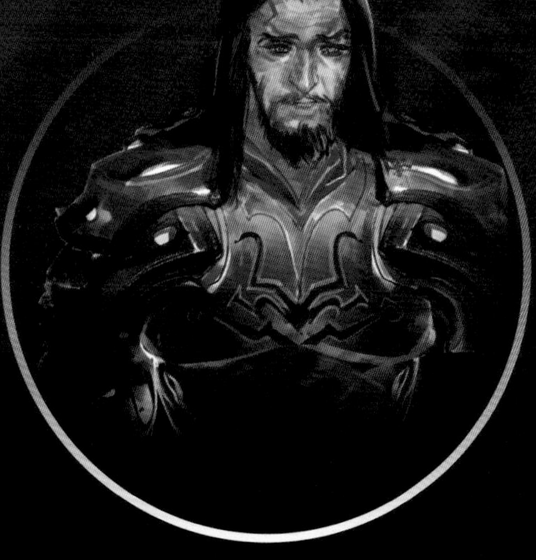

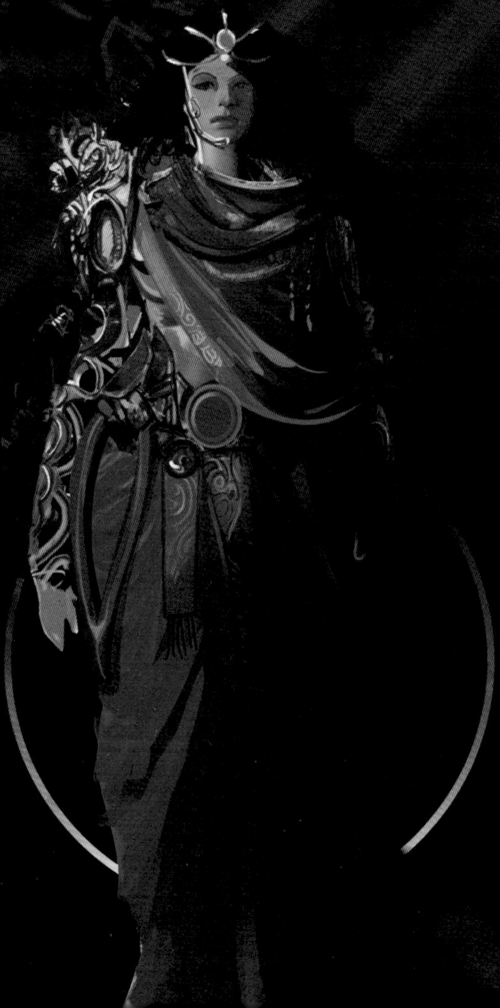

DUSASANA

Prince Dusasana is Duryodhana's favourite brother, and the father of Durmashana. If anything, the Pandavas hate him even more than they hate Duryodhana. In the past, Dusasana is reported to have humiliated and assaulted the Pandava Queen, Draupadi, and they are determined to make him pay for his crime. Bheema, the wildest of the Pandava brothers has sworn to tear Dusasana's heart from his chest and eat it. Dusasana in turn has hated Bheema since their early teens when he was often the victim of his cousin's bullying.

THE KAURAVA EMPIRE

RE-IMAGINING THE GREATEST STORIES EVER TOLD

The villains were not cardboard cut-out villainous people, but real people, likewise the heroes were not holier than thou paragons of virtue, they too were real, complete with faults. In fact, what really got to me was that the villains seemed in many ways no worse than the heroes, the heroes no better than the villains.

When I first arrived in Delhi as Creative Content Head at Campfire Graphic Novels, the first thing I had to do was catch up on all of Campfire's back titles. Now as a life-long fan of the medium, who learned to read with comic books, this was no great hardship. I devoured the books in our Classics list, I zipped through the biographies in our Heroes list, I read the Originals and then came to the Mythology titles. Now, I was already familiar with the tales of Zeus, Hercules, Jason and the Argonauts, and the others in the pantheon of ancient Greek heroes but I was pretty unfamiliar with most of the Hindu tales. Sure, I knew who Krishna was, but I had no idea what he actually did, and as for Draupadi, Sita, Ravana, Hanuman, and the others, I could barely pronounce their names let alone have any clue as to their actual stories.

To help me get a better grip on these characters I began reading the Mahabharata, (not in Sanskrit, I confess, but in English) and I was blown away. The characters didn't seem like dusty relics from the past, they seemed real, with real problems, real passions.

Duryodhana, the main villain of the piece is capable of acts of great kindness, generosity and friendship. Arjuna, one of the great heroes, is also capable of acts of arrogance and meanness. I found myself falling in love with these characters, and I could understand those who fought on the Kaurava side in the great war. They weren't all fighting for Duryodhana because they were evil or because they loved evil, but because they loved order, they loved Duryodhana and his family.

There is no black and white in the Mahabharata, simply many, many shades of grey. I found myself equally enamoured with both sides, both the Kauravas and the Pandavas and I began thinking about our next book. I began thinking of a series of books.

The Mahabharata is massive. But it contains hundreds, no thousands of great stories, and great characters. Rather than trying to cram everything into one short graphic novel, we decided to opt for different episodes, different standalone stories. Many of the characters would develop from book to book, many would appear throughout each story, but each book could be read as a standalone book.

My key objective when writing the first volume in this series was to bring these stories to the world. Obviously, the vast majority of Indians are already familiar with the story of the Pandavas and the Kauravas, so I wanted to give them something new, and I wanted to attract people from other parts of the world too, to excite them in the same way I had been excited. Anyone who loves *Game of Thrones*, or *Lord of the Rings*, would love these stories. I'll risk the ire of long-term fans of both those series and say the tales of the Mahabharata are in a different league, so if you liked those books you are going to absolutely love this.

For me, the ideas, the passions, the intrigues that run through the Mahabharata are timeless and I wanted to present them in a way that reflects the timeless nature of the original. This is why we have gone 'space-age'. We haven't changed the story. The story is exactly the same, we have simply shifted the setting slightly.

The next big question facing us was which story do we kick the series off with? I really wanted to show the beginning of the enmity between the Kauravas and their Pandava cousins, to show the seeds of the great trouble to come, but then decided to hold that in reserve and kick off with a real all-out action blockbuster. The story of Abhimanyu was perfect. We've got a teen-age hero, we've got sacrifice, we've got impossible odds, we've got heartbreak and we've got lots and lots of action.

Abhimanyu really is a superhero. He's an expert warrior, he's brave and reckless, and he wants to prove himself. His father Arjun has long been touted as the greatest warrior in the world and that can be a big shadow for a teenager. Abhimanyu wants to prove himself and he gets his chance on the battlefield of Kurukshetra when only his sacrifice can save his family from annihilation.

So, we now had our first episode, next we needed an artist and for me there was only one choice, the incomparable Sachin Nagar. Sachin was just putting the finishing touches to *Gandhi: My Life is My Message*, and before that he had completed *Mother Teresa: Angel of the Slums*. The artwork in both of those books is exquisite. Every page has something you want to pull out and frame on your wall. Sachin is one of those artists who is always seeking to push himself, to try new things. He didn't want to do another biography, not after Gandhi and Mother Teresa. He wanted something with action and imagination. I like to tell myself he's happy with the script I gave him because the work he has done on this book surpasses everything he's done before and that really is saying something.

The Kaurava Empire has been a labour of love for all the team and I really hope you will share our excitement about this book and this series, because I've got a feeling we're in at the start of something very special.

JASON QUINN
DELHI,
MAY 2014